EASY SPANISH PHRASE BOOK

Over 1500 Common Phrases
For Everyday Use And Travel

Lingo Mastery

www.LingoMastery.com

Free Book Reveals The 6 Step Blueprint That Took Students
<u>From Language Learners To Fluent In 3 Months</u>

- **6 Unbelievable Hacks** that will accelerate your learning curve
- **Mind Training:** why memorizing vocabulary is easy
- **One Hack To Rule Them All:** This <u>secret nugget</u> will blow you away...

CONTENTS

INTRODUCTION

If you have finally decided to visit one of the most beautiful countries in the world, then you can't help but consider the words, phrases, ways of saying that you will use in certain situations, which you must know before leaving.

Thanks to this book, we will see how to deal with many situations that can be simple, complicated, funny or even not funny at all. All those real situations that a tourist will experience when, for example, they want to drink a coffee, order a good *paella*, or simply tell the waiter that what they have just eaten has not been to their liking.

Think of the souvenirs to bring back to a relative. Do you want to negotiate on the price or ask for a discount? It is certainly here that you will need to find the way to express yourself correctly.

Most of the time, a translation with the vocabulary at your fingertips is the best solution and therefore, why not take precautions and study a few phrases that could amaze your fellow travelers or your interlocutors?

Of course, there are some obstacles to overcome. Let's see for example what can create difficulties at a phonetic level in the Spanish language.

How to pronounce the Spanish vowels

There are five vowels in the Spanish language: A, E, I, O, U.

Each vowel has only one pronunciation. There are strong and weak vowels in the Spanish language.

Strong vowels require the speaker to open their mouth more in order to pronounce them properly. Strong vowels are **a, e, o.**

On the other hand, *weak vowels* do not require an important opening of the mouth. Weak vowels are **i, u.**

In the Spanish language, vowels have a regular length and their sounds are usually shorter than the pronunciation of English vowels. Remember, there are only five sound vowels in Spanish; this will facilitate your improvement in pronunciation!

The vowel A

The Spanish "a" sound resembles the "a" in father but is just a little bit wider. You must pronounce it only in this way.

Amor (love)
Ala (wing)
Árbol (tree)
Año (year)
Cáncer (cancer)
Habrá (there will be)

When a vowel is marked with an accent, it means that you must add emphasis on that syllable as you speak it. However, the vowels don't get longer or shorter, pronunciation does not vary.

The vowel E

The sound of the vowel "E" in Spanish is like the first "e" in the English word "elephant". The vowel "e" will always sound like that.

Elemento (element)
Espejo (mirror)
Economía (economy)

The vowel I

To pronounce correctly the vowel "i" you need to make the sound of the double "e" in English. The sound of the "i" resembles the "ee" in "bee", or "cheek", but is shorter and more concise.

Iglesia (church)
Colibrí (hummingbird)

The vowel O

The "O" vowel sounds like the first "o" in the British pronunciation of "October".

Oso (bear)
Otro (other)

The vowel U

The Spanish "u" sounds like the double "o" in English. However, remember that "u" is a single vowel, hence, the sounds are shorter.

Uva (grapes)
Universidad (university)

Pronunciation of vowel combination

Whenever you find a vowel combination in the Spanish language, remember that you must pronounce all vowels. Here you'll find a few examples:

The vowel combination AA

AA, as a long "a" in "father". This combination however is very uncommon.
Áaron
Contraataque

The vowel combination AE

AE, ah eh
Cae

The vowel combination AI

AI, pronounced as "eye"
Aire

The vowel combination AO

AO, ah oh
Chao

The vowel combination AU

AU, ah oo
Audición

The vowel combination EA

EA, eh ah
Patea

The vowel combination EE

EE, pronounced as a long "eh" sound
Cree

The vowel combination EI

EI, eh ee
Aceite

The vowel combination EO

EO, eh oh
Aseo

The vowel combination EU

EU, eh oo
Europa

The vowel combination IA

IA, ee ah
Abría

The vowel combination IE

IE, ee eh
Alien

The vowel combination II

II, a long "ee" sound
Antiinflamatorio

The vowel combination IO

IO, ee oh
Odio

The vowel combination IU

IU, ee oo
Viuda

The vowel combination OA

OA, oh ah
Oasis

The vowel combination OE

OE, oh eh
Poema

The vowel combination OI

OI, oh ee
Boina

The vowel combination OO

OO, oh
Zoológico

The vowel combination UA

UA, oo ah
Agua

The vowel combination UE

UE, oo eh
Hueso

The vowel combination UI

UI, oo ee
Cuidado

The vowel combination UO

UO, oo oh
Licuo

How to pronounce the Spanish consonants

Now that we've seen the Spanish vowels, it's time to look at how consonants behave. Most consonants are pronounced as in English; however, you must be careful with a few of them.

Let's see the important consonants in detail.

The consonant C

The pronunciation of the Spanish consonant C will vary depending on the vowel following it.

C + a, o, u.

When the letter C is followed by the vowels "a", "o" or "u", it is pronounced using the sound of the letter "K".

Examples:
Casa (house) (kah-sah)
Color (color) (koh-lohr)
Cuchillo (knife) (kuh-chee-yoh)

C + e, i.

When the letter C is followed by the vowel "e", and "i" the pronunciation changes and the sound resembles the pronunciation of the English consonant "S".

Examples:

Ceja (eyebrow) (seh-hah)
Ciudad (city) (see-oo-dahd)

C + H

"CH" is the combination of two letters, the pronunciation resembles the sound of the "ch" in most English words such as "chick", "champion" or "charm".

Examples:
Chica (chee-kah)

The consonant G

The consonant G follows the same rules of C, so:

G + a, o , u

It behaves like the "g" in "game".

Examples:
Gato (cat) (gah-toh)
Gusano (worm) (goo-sah-noh)

G + e, i.

It is pronounced like the Spanish "j" (which has the same sound of the English "h" in "hello").

Examples:
Gema (gem) (heh-mah)

Now let's get into a more complex combination. Some words in Spanish have a G+ui, ue combination. In both cases you can ignore the "u" and then pronounce the "g" as the "g" in "game".

Example:
Guerra (war) (geh-rrah)
Guiso (stew) (gee-soh)

There's an exception. In words like "pingüino" you'll see a diaeresis. This symbol indicates that you must pronounce the vowel "u". Again, "g" will behave like the "g" in "game".

Example:
Pingüino (penguin) (peen-goo-ee-noh)

The consonant H

Unlike English, the Spanish H at the beginning of a word is always silent. Remember, if you see the consonant H in words like "hormiga" (ohr-mee-gah), "hotel" (oh-tehl), you can ignore it since it has no sound.

Pronouncing LL

As the "y" in "yes".

Example:
Lluvia (rain) (yoo-vee-ah)

The consonant Ñ

Ñ, the letter you'll find only in the Spanish alphabet. The correct pronunciation of the letter Ñ (eh-nyeh) is similar to the English sound *NY*.

Now that you're more familiar with the sound, here's a tip to achieve a perfect pronunciation:

Place your tongue on your palate, as if you were going to pronounce the consonant N, but instead of using only the tip, use your whole tongue.

Examples:
Español (Spanish) (ehs-pah-nyohl)
Niña (girl) (nee-nyah)

The consonant P

It's never aspirated. The Spanish P will always sound like the "P" in English words "page", or "painter".

The consonant Q

Like the English "k"! It is always written before an "ue" or "ui" combination.

Examples:
Queso (cheese) (keh-soh)

*Note: you can ignore the "u", as it is never pronounced between the letter "q" and another vowel.

The consonant R

There are two possible ways to pronounce the R, a strong one and a soft one. Here are some basic rules that will guide you:

Double "r": strong pronunciation, it requires the vibration of the tip of the tongue against your palate, just at the back of the teeth but without touching them.

Example:
Perro (dog) (peh-rroh)

Single "r": soft sound. Tip: the single "r" sound resembles the faint "d" sound that results from pronouncing "butter" or "water" with an

American accent. See if you can roll the tip of your tongue starting with that sound!

Example:

Pera (pear) (peh-rah)

The consonant T

Always pronounce it as the "t" in "tomorrow".

COLORS

Gold
Dorado
Doh-RAH-doh

Blue
Azul
Ah-SOOL

Purple
Morado
Moh-RAH-doh

Red
Rojo
RROH-hoh

Light blue
Azul claro
Ah-SOOL KLAH-roh

White
Blanco
BLAHN-koh

Orange
Naranja
Nah-RAHN-hah

Violet
Violeta
Vee-oh-LEH-tah

Black
Negro
NEH-groh

Yellow
Amarillo
Ah-mah-REE-yoh

Pink
Rosado
FOOK-see-ah RO-sah-doh

Gray
Gris
Grees

Green
Verde
VEHR-deh

Brown
Marrón
Mah-RROHN

Silver
Plateado
Plah-teh-AH-doh

What color is that sign?
¿De qué color es esa señal?
Deh keh koh-LOHR ehs EH-sah seh-NYAHL

Is the cartoon in color?
¿La caricatura es a color?
Lah kah-ree-kah-TOO-rah ehs ah koh-LOHR

Is this television show in color?
¿Este programa de televisión es a color?
EHS-teh proh-GRAH-mah deh teh-leh-vee-see-OHN ehs ah koh-LOHR

This is a red pen.
Este es un bolígrafo rojo.
EHS-teh ehs oon boh-LEE-grah-foh RROH-hoh

This piece of paper is blue.
Este pedazo de papel es azul.
EHS-teh peh-DAH-soh deh pah-PEHL ehs ah-SOOL

What color is that car?
¿De qué color es ese auto?
Deh keh koh-LOHR ehs EH-seh AH-oo-toh

What color are your clothes?
¿De qué color es tu ropa?
Deh keh koh-LOHR ehs too RROH-pah

Is this the right color?
¿Es este el color correcto?
Ehs EHS-teh ehl koh-LOHR koh-RREHK-toh

What color is the stop light?
¿De qué color es el semáforo?
Deh keh koh-LOHR ehs ehl seh-MAH-foh-roh

Does that color mean danger?
¿Ese color significa peligro?
EH-seh koh-LOHR seeg-nee-FEE-kah peh-LEE-groh

That bird is red.
El pájaro es rojo.
Ehl PAH-hah-roh ehs RROH-hoh

What color is that animal?
¿De qué color es ese animal?
Deh keh koh-LOHR ehs EH-seh ah-nee-mahl

The sky is blue.
El cielo es azul.
Ehl see-EH-loh ehs ah-SOOL

The clouds are white.
Las nubes son blancas.
Lahs NOO-behs sohn BLAHN-kahs

That paint is blue.
La pintura es azul.
Lah peen-TOO-rah ehs ah-SOOL

Press the red button.
Presiona el botón rojo.
Preh-see-OH-nah ehl boh-TOHN RROH-hoh

Don't press the red button.
No presiones el botón rojo.
Noh preh-see-OH-nehs ehl boh-TOHN RROH-hoh

Black and white
Blanco y negro
BLAHN-koh ee NEH-groh

Look at all the colors.
Mira todos los colores.
MEE-rah TOH-dohs lohs koh-LOH-rehs

Is that a color television?
¿Ése es un televisor a color?
EH-seh ehs oon teh-leh-vee-SOHR ah koh-LOHR

What color do you see?
¿Qué color ves?
Keh koh-LOHR vehs

Can I have the color blue?
¿Me das el color azul?
Meh dahs ehl koh-LOHR ah-SOOL

What color do you have for these frames?
¿Qué colores tienes para éstos marcos?
Keh koh-LOH-rehs tee-EH-nehs PAH-rah EHS-tohs MAHR-kohs

Don't go until the color is green.
No vayas hasta que el color sea verde.
Noh VAH-yahs AS-tah keh ehl koh-LOHR SEH-ah VEHR-deh

Coloring pencils.
Lápices de colores.
LAH-pee-sehs deh koh-LOH-rehs

Coloring pens.
Bolígrafos de colores.
Boh-LEE-grah-fohs deh koh-LOH-rehs

The sharpie is black.
El marcador es negro.
Ehl mahr-kah-DOHR ehs NEH-groh

I passed with flying colors.
Me gradué con honores.
Meh grah-doo-EH kohn oh-NOH-rehs

Do you have this in another color?
¿Tienes esto en otro color?
Tee-EH-nehs EHS-toh ehn OH-troh koh-LOHR

Do you have this in a darker color?
¿Tienes esto en un color más oscuro?
Tee-EH-nehs EHS-toh ehn oon koh-LOHR mahs ohs-KOO-roh

Do you have this in a lighter color?
¿Tienes esto en un color más claro?
Tee-EH-nehs EHS-toh ehn oon koh-LOHR mahs KLAH-roh

Can you paint my house blue?
¿Puedes pintar mi casa de azul?
PWEH-dehs peen-TAHR mee KAH-sah deh ah-SOOL

Can you paint my car the same color?
¿Puedes pintar mi auto del mismo color?
PWEH-dehs peen-TAHR mee AH-oo-toh dehl MEES-moh koh-LOHR

The flag has three different colors.
La bandera tiene tres colores diferentes.
Lah bahn-DEH-rah tee-EH-neh trehs koh-LOH-rehs dee-feh-REHN-tehs

Is the color on the flag red?
¿El color en la bandera es rojo?
Ehl koh-LOHR ehn lah bahn-DEH-rah ehs RROH-hoh

NUMBERS

Zero
Cero
SEH-roh

One
Uno
OO-noh

Two
Dos
Dohs

Three
Tres
Trehs

Four
Cuatro
KWAH-troh

Five
Cinco
SEEN-koh

Six
Seis
SEH-ees

Seven
Siete
See-EH-teh

Eight
Ocho
OH-choh

Nine
Nueve
NWEH-veh

Ten
Diez
Dee-EHS

Eleven
Once
OHN-seh

Twelve
Doce
DOH-seh

Thirteen
Trece
TREH-seh

Fourteen
Catorce
Kah-TOHR-seh

Fifteen
Quince
KEEN-seh

Sixteen
Dieciséis
Dee-eh-see-SEH-ees

Seventeen
Diecisiete
Dee-eh-see-see-EH-teh

Eighteen
Dieciocho
Dee-eh-see-OH-choh

Nineteen
Diecinueve
Dee-eh-see-NWEH-veh

Twenty
Veinte
VEH-een-teh

Twenty-one
Veintiuno
Veh-een-tee-OO-noh

Twenty-two
Veintidós
Veh-een-tee-DOHS

Twenty-three
Veintitrés
Veh-een-tee-TREHS

Twenty-four
Veinticuatro
Veh-een-tee-KWAH-troh

Twenty-five
Veinticinco
Veh-een-tee-SEEN-koh

Twenty-six
Veintiséis
Veh-een-tee-SEH-ees

Twenty-seven
Veintisiete
Veh-een-tee-see-EH-teh

Twenty-eighth
Veintiocho
Veh-een-tee-OH-choh

Twenty-nine
Veintinueve
Veh-een-tee-NWEH-veh

Thirty
Treinta
TREH-een-tah

Forty
Cuarenta
Kwah-REHN-tah

Fifty
Cincuenta
Seen-KWEHN-tah

Sixty
Sesenta
Seh-SEHN-tah

Seventy
Setenta
Seh-TEHN-tah

Eighty
Ochenta
Oh-CHEHN-tah

Ninety
Noventa
Noh-VEHN-tah

One-hundred
Cien

See-EHN

Two-hundred
Doscientos
Dohs-see-EHN-tos

Five-hundred
Quinientos
Kee-nee-EHN-tohs

One-thousand
Mil
Meel

One-hundred-thousand
Cien mil

See-EHN meel

One million
Un millón
Oon mee-YOHN

One billion
Un billón
Oon bee-YOHN

What does that add up to?
¿Cuánto suma eso?
KWAHN-toh SOO-mah EH-soh

What number is on this paper?
¿Qué número hay en este papel?
Keh NOO-meh-roh AH-ee ehn EHS-teh pah-PEHL

What number is on this sign?
¿Qué número hay en esta señal?
Keh NOO-meh-roh AH-ee ehn EHS-tah seh-NYAHL

Are these two numbers equal?
¿Estos dos números son iguales?
EHS-tohs dohs NOO-meh-rohs sohn ee-goo-AH-lehs

My social security number is one, two, three, four, five.
Mi número de seguridad social es uno, dos, tres, cuatro, cinco.
Mee NOO-meh-roh deh seh-goo-ree-DAHD soh-see-AHL ehs OO-noh,
dohs, trehs, KWAH-troh, SEEN-koh

I'm going to bet five-thousand Euros.
Voy a apostar cinco mil euros.
VOH-ee ah ah-pohs-TAHR SEEN-koh meel EH-oo-rohs

Can you count to one hundred for me?
¿Puedes contar hasta cien para mí?
PWEH-dehs kohn-TAHR AHS-tah see-EHN PAH-rah mee

I took fourteen steps.
Di catorce pasos.
Dee kah-TOHR-seh PAH-sohs

I ran two kilometers.
Corrí dos kilómetros.
Koh-RREE dohs kee-LOH-meh-trohs

The speed limit is 30 km/h.
El límite de velocidad es treinta kilómetros por hora.

Ehl LEE-mee-teh deh veh-loh-see-DAHD ehs TREH-een-tah kee-LOH-
meh-trohs pohr OH-rah

What are the measurements?
¿Cuáles son las medidas?
KWAH-lehs sohn lahs meh-DEE-dahs

Can you dial this number?
¿Puedes marcar este número?
PWEH-dehs mahr-KAHR EHS-teh NOO-meh-roh

One dozen.
Una docena.
OO-nah doh-SEH-nah

A half dozen.
Media docena.
MEH-dee-ah doh-SEH-nah

How many digits are in the number?
¿Cuántos dígitos hay en el número?
KWAHN-tohs DEE-hee-tohs AH-ee ehn ehl NOO-meh-roh

My phone number is nine, eight, five, six, two, one, eight, seven, eight, eight.
Mi número telefónico es nueve, ocho, cinco, seis, dos, uno, ocho, siete, ocho, ocho.
Mee NOO-meh-roh teh-leh-FOH-nee-koh ehs NWEH-veh, OH-choh, SEEN-koh, SEH-ees, dohs, OO-noh, OH-choh, see-EH-teh, OH-choh, OH-choh.

The hotel's phone number is one, eight-hundred, three, two, three, five, seven, five, five.
El número telefónico del hotel es uno, ochocientos, tres, dos, tres, cinco, siete, cinco, cinco.
Ehl NOO-meh-roh teh-leh-FOH-nee-koh dehl oh-TEHL ehs OO-noh, oh-choh-see-EHN-tohs, trehs, dohs, trehs, SEEN-koh, see-EH-teh, SEEN-koh, SEEN-koh.

The taxi number is six, eight, one, four, four, four, five, eight, one, nine.
El número para llamar el taxi es seis, ocho, uno, cuatro, cuatro, cuatro, cinco, ocho, uno, nueve.

Ehl NOO-meh-roh PAH-rah yah-MAHR ehl TAK-see ehs SEH-ees, OH-choh, OO-noh, KWAH-troh, KWAH-troh, KWAH-troh, SEEN-koh, OH-choh, OO-noh, NWEH-veh.

Call my hotel at two, one, four, seven, one, two, nine, five, seven, six.
Llama a mi hotel al dos, uno, cuatro, siete, uno, dos, nueve, cinco, siete, seis.

YAH-mah ah mee oh-TEHL ahl dohs, OO-noh, KWAH-troh, see-EH-teh, OO-noh, dohs, NWEH-veh, SEEN-koh, see-EH-teh, SEH-ees.

Call the embassy at nine, eight, nine, eight, four, three, two, one, seven, one.
Llama a la embajada al nueve, ocho, nueve, ocho, cuatro, tres, dos, uno, siete, uno.
YAH-mah ah lah ehm-bah-HAH-dah ahl NWEH-veh, OH-choh, NWEH-veh, OH-choh, KWAH-troh, trehs, dohs, OO-noh, see-EH-teh, OO-noh.

GREETINGS

Hello!
¡Hola!
OH-lah

How's it going?
¿Cómo estás?
KOH-moh ehs-TAHS

What's new?
¿Qué hay de nuevo?
Keh AH-ee deh NWEH-voh

What's going on?
¿Qué pasa?
Keh PAH-sah

Home, sweet home.
Hogar, dulce hogar.
Oh-GAHR, DOOL-seh oh-GAHR

Ladies and gentlemen, thank you for coming.
Damas y caballeros, gracias por venir.
DAH-mahs ee kah-bah-YEH-rohs, GRAH-see-ahs pohr veh-NEER

How is everything?
¿Cómo está todo?
KOH-moh ehs-TAH TOH-doh

Long time no see.
Tiempo sin verte.
Tee-EHM-poh seen VEHR-teh

It's been a long time.
Ha pasado mucho tiempo.
Ah pah-SAH-doh MOO-choh tee-EHM-poh

It's been a while!
¡Ha pasado un tiempo!
Ah pah-SAH-doh oon tee-EHM-poh

How is life?
¿Cómo va tu vida?
KOH-moh vah too VEE-dah

How is your day?
¿Qué tal tu día?
Keh tahl too DEE-ah

Good morning.
Buenos días.

BWEH-nohs DEE-ahs

It's been too long!
¡Ha pasado demasiado tiempo!
Ah pah-SAH-doh deh-mah-see-AH-doh tee-EHM-poh

Good afternoon.
Buenas tardes.

BWEH-nahs TAHR-dehs

How long has it been?
¿Cuánto tiempo ha pasado?
KWAHN-toh tee-EHM-poh ah pah-SAH-doh

It's a pleasure to meet you.
Es un placer conocerte.
Ehs oon plah-SEHR koh-noh-SEHR-teh

It's always a pleasure to see you.
Siempre es un placer verte.
See-EHM-preh ehs oon plah-SEHR VEHR-teh

Allow me to introduce Earl, my husband.
Permíteme presentarte a mi esposo, Earl.
Pehr-MEE-teh-meh preh-sehn-TAHR-teh ah mee ehs-POH-soh, Earl.

Goodnight.
Buenas noches.
BWEH-nahs NOH-chehs

May I introduce my brother and sister?
¿Puedo presentarte a mi hermano y hermana?
PWEH-doh preh-sehn-TAHR-teh ah mee ehr-MAH-noh ee ehr-MAH-nah

Good evening.
Buenas noches.
BWEH-nahs NOH-chehs

What's happening?
¿Qué está pasando?
Keh ehs-TAH pah-SAHN-doh

Happy holidays!
¡Felices fiestas!
Feh-LEE-sehs fee-EHS-tahs

Are you alright?
¿Estás bien?
Ehs-TAHS bee-EHN

Merry Christmas!
¡Feliz navidad!
Feh-LEES nah-vee-DAHD

Where have you been hiding?
¿Dónde te has estado escondiendo?
DOHN-deh teh ahs ehs-TAH-doh ehs-kohn-dee-EHN-doh

Happy New Year!
¡Feliz Año Nuevo!
Feh-LEES AH-nyoh NWEH-voh

How is your night?
¿Cómo va tu noche?
KOH-moh vah too NOH-cheh

What have you been up to all these years?
¿En qué has estado todos estos años?
Ehn keh ahs ehs-TAH-doh TOH-dohs EHS-tohs AH-nyohs

When was the last time we saw each other?
¿Cuándo fue la última vez que nos vimos?
KWAHN-doh foo-EH lah OOL-tee-mah vehs keh nohs VEE-mohs

It's been ages since I've seen you.
Han pasado años desde la última vez que te vi.
Ahn pah-SAH-doh AH-nyohs DEHS-deh lah OOL-tee-mah vehs keh teh vee

How have things been going since I saw you last?
¿Cómo te ha ido desde la última vez que te vi?
KOH-moh teh ah EE-doh DEHS-deh lah OOL-tee-mah vehs keh teh vee

What have you been up to?
¿Qué has estado haciendo?
Keh ahs EHS-ta-do ah-cien-doh

How are you doing?
¿Cómo te va?
KOH-moh teh vah

Goodbye.
Adiós.
Ah-dee-OHS

Are you okay?
¿Estás bien?
Ehs-TAHS bee-EHN

How's life been treating you?
¿Cómo te ha tratado la vida?
KOH-moh teh ah trah-TAH-doh lah VEE-dah

I'm sorry.
Lo siento.
Loh see-EHN-toh

Excuse me.
Disculpa.
Dees-KOOL-pah

See you later!
¡Te veo luego!
Teh VEH-oh loo-EH-goh

What's your name?
¿Cómo te llamas?
KOH-moh teh YAH-mahs

My name is Bill.
Mi nombre es Bill.
Mee NOHM-breh ehs Bill

Pleased to meet you.
Encantado de conocerte.
Ehn-kahn-TAH-doh deh koh-noh-SEHR-teh

How do you do?
¿Cómo vas?
KOH-moh vahs

How are things?
¿Cómo están las cosas?
KOH-moh ehs-TAHN lahs KOH-sahs

You're welcome.
De nada.
Deh NAH-dah

It's good to see you.
Es bueno verte.
Ehs BWEH-noh VEHR-teh

Nice to meet you.
Mucho gusto.
MOO-choh GOOS-toh

Fine, thanks. And you?
Bien, gracias. ¿Y tú?
Bee-EHN, GRAH-see-ahs. Ee too

Good day to you.
Buen día para tí.
Bwehn DEE-ah pah-rah tee

Come in, the door is open.
Adelante, la puerta está abierta.
Ah-deh-LAHN-teh lah PWEHR-tah ehs-TAH ah-bee-EHR-tah

My wife's name is Sheila.
El nombre de mi esposa es Sheila.
Ehl NOHM-breh deh mee ehs-POH-sah ehs Sheila

I've been looking for you!
¡He estado buscándote!
Eh ehs-TAH-doh boos-KAHN-doh-teh

Allow me to introduce myself. My name is Earl.
Permíteme presentarme. Mi nombre es Earl.
Pehr-MEE-teh-meh preh-sehn-TAHR-meh. Mee NOHM-breh ehs Earl

I hope you have enjoyed your weekend!
¡Espero que hayas disfrutado tu fin de semana!
Ehs-PEH-roh keh AH-yahs dees-froo-TAH-doh too feen deh seh-MAH-nah

It's great to hear from you.
¡Qué bueno saber de ti!
Keh BWEH-noh sah-BEHR deh tee

I hope you are having a great day.
Espero que estés teniendo un gran día.
Ehs-PEH-roh keh ehs-TEHS teh-nee-EHN-doh oon grahn DEE-ah

Thank you for your help.
Gracias por tu ayuda.
GRAH-see-ahs pohr too ah-YOO-dah

DATE AND TIME

January
Enero
Eh-NEH-roh

February
Febrero
Feh-BREH-roh

March
Marzo
MAHR-soh

April
Abril
Ah-BREEL

May
Mayo
MAH-yoh

June
Junio
HOO-nee-oh

July
Julio
HOO-lee-oh

August
Agosto
Ah-GOHS-toh

September
Septiembre
Sehp-tee-EHM-breh

October
Octubre
Ohk-TOO-breh

November
Noviembre
Noh-vee-EHM-breh

December
Diciembre
Dee-see-EHM-breh

What month is it?
¿Qué mes es este?
Keh mehs ehs EHS-teh

At what time?
¿A qué hora?
Ah keh OH-rah

Do you observe daylight savings time?
¿Ustedes siguen el horario de verano?
Oos-TEH-dehs SEE-gehn ehl oh-RAH-ree-oh deh veh-RAH-noh

The current month is January.
Este mes es enero.
EHS-teh mehs ehs eh-NEH-roh

What day of the week is it?
¿Qué día es hoy?
Keh DEE-ah ehs OH-ee

Is today Tuesday?
¿Hoy es jueves?
OH-ee ehs hoo-EH-vehs

Today is Monday.
Hoy es lunes.
OH-ee ehs LOO-nehs

Is this the month of January?
¿Este mes es enero?
EHS-teh mehs ehs eh-NEH-roh

It is five minutes past one.
Es la una y cinco minutos.
Ehs lah OO-nah ee SEEN-koh mee-NOO-tohs

It is ten minutes past one.
Es la una y diez minutos.
Ehs lah OO-nah ee dee-EHS mee-NOO-tohs

It is ten till one.
Faltan diez para la una.
FAHL-tahn dee-EHS PAH-rah lah OO-nah

It is half past one.
Es la una y media.
Ehs lah OO-nah ee MEH-dee-ah

What time is it?
¿Qué hora es?
Keh OH-rah ehs?

When does the sun go down?
¿A qué hora se pone el sol?
Ah keh OH-rah seh POH-neh ehl sohl

It's the third of November.
Hoy es tres de noviembre.
OH-ee ehs trehs deh noh-vee-EHM-breh

When does it get dark?
¿A qué hora oscurece?
Ah keh OH-rah ohs-koo-REH-seh

What is today's date?
¿Qué fecha es hoy?
Keh FEH-chah ehs OH-ee

What time does the shoe store open?
¿A qué hora abre la tienda de zapatos?
Ah keh OH-rah AH-breh lah tee-EHN-dah deh sah-PAH-tohs

Is today a holiday?
¿Hoy es un día festivo?
OH-ee ehs oon DEE-ah fehs-TEE-voh

When is the next holiday?
¿Cuándo es el próximo día festivo?
KWAHN-doh ehs ehl PROHK-see-moh DEE-ah fehs-TEE-voh

I will meet you at noon.
Te veré al mediodía.
Teh veh-REH ahl meh-dee-oh-DEE-ah

I will meet you later tonight.
Nos veremos en la noche.
Nohs veh-REH-mohs ehn lah NOH-cheh

My appointment is in ten minutes.
Mi cita es en diez minutos.
Mee SEE-tah ehs ehn dee-EHS mee-NOO-tohs

Can we meet in half an hour?
¿Podemos vernos en media hora?
Poh-DEH-mohs VEHR-nohs ehn MEH-dee-ah OH-rah

I will see you in March.
Te veré en marzo.
Teh veh-REH ehn MAHR-soh

The meeting is scheduled for the twelfth.
La reunión está programada para el doce.
Lah rreh-oo-nee-OHN ehs-TAH proh-grah-MAH-dah PAH-rah ehl DOH-seh

Can we set up the meeting for noon tomorrow?
¿Podemos programar la reunión para mañana al mediodía?
Poh-DEH-mohs proh-grah-MAHR lah rreh-oo-nee-OHN PAH-rah mah-NYAH-nah ahl meh-dee-oh-DEE-ah

What time will the cab arrive?
¿A qué hora llegará el taxi?
Ah keh OH-rah yeh-gah-RAH ehl TAK-see

Can you be here by midnight?
¿Puedes estar aquí a la medianoche?
PWEH-dehs ehs-TAHR ah-KEE ah lah meh-dee-ah-NOH-cheh

The grand opening is scheduled for three o'clock.
La gran apertura está programada para las tres en punto.
Lah grahn ah-pehr-TOO-rah ehs-TAH proh-grah-MAH-dah PAH-rah lahs trehs ehn POON-toh

When is your birthday?
¿Cuándo es tu cumpleaños?
KWAHN-doh ehs too koom-pleh-AH-nyohs

My birthday is on the second of June.
Mi cumpleaños es el dos de junio.
Mee koom-pleh-AH-nyohs ehs ehl dohs deh HOO-nee-oh

This place opens at ten a.m.
Este lugar abre a las diez de la mañana
EHS-teh loo-GAHR AH-breh ah lahs dee-EHS deh lah mah-NYAH-nah

From what time?
¿Desde qué hora?
DEHS-deh keh OH-rah

Sorry, it is already too late at night.
Lo siento, ya es muy tarde en la noche
Loh see-EHN-toh yah ehs MOO-ee TAHR-deh ehn lah NOH-cheh

COMMON QUESTIONS

Do you speak English?
¿Hablas inglés?
AH-blahs een-GLEHS

What is your hobby?
¿Cuál es tu pasatiempo?
Kwahl ehs too pah-sah-tee-EHM-poh

What language do you speak?
¿Qué idioma hablas?
Keh ee-dee-OH-mah AH-blahs

Was it hard?
¿Fue difícil?
Foo-EH dee-FEE-seel

Can you help me?
¿Puedes ayudarme?
PWEH-dehs ah-yoo-DAHR-meh

Where can I find help?
¿Dónde puedo encontrar ayuda?
DOHN-deh PWEH-doh ehn-kohn-TRAHR ah-YOO-dah

Where are we right now?
¿Dónde estamos ahora mismo?
DOHN-deh ehs-TAH-mohs ah-OH-rah MEES-moh

Where were you last night?
¿Dónde estuviste anoche?

DOHN-deh ehs-too-VEES-teh ah-NOH-cheh

What type of a tree is that?
¿Qué tipo de árbol es ese?
Keh TEE-poh deh AHR-bohl ehs EH-seh

Do you plan on coming back here again?
¿Planeas volver aquí otra vez?
Plah-NEH-ahs vohl-VEHR ah-KEE OH-trah vehs

What kind of an animal is that?
¿Qué clase de animal es ese?
Keh KLAH-seh deh ah-nee-MAHL ehs EH-se

Is that animal dangerous?
¿Es peligroso ese animal?
Ehs peh-lee-GROH-soh EH-seh ah-nee-MAHL

Is it available?
¿Está disponible?
Ehs-TAH dees-poh-NEE-bleh

Can we come see it?
¿Podemos ir a verlo?
Poh-DEH-mohs eer ah VEHR-loh

Where do you live?
¿Dónde vives?
DOHN-deh VEE-vehs

Earl, what city are you from?
Earl, ¿de qué ciudad eres?
Earl, deh keh see-oo-DAHD EH-rehs

Is it a very large city?
¿Es una ciudad muy grande?
Ehs OO-nah see-oo-DAHD MOO-ee GRAHN-deh

Is there another available bathroom?
¿Hay otro baño disponible?
AH-ee OH-troh BAH-nyoh dees-poh-NEE-bleh

How was your trip?
¿Cómo estuvo tu viaje?
KOH-moh ehs-TOO-voh too vee-AH-heh

Is the bathroom free?
¿El baño es gratuito?
Ehl BAH-nyoh ehs grah-too-EE-toh

How are you feeling?
¿Cómo te sientes?
KOH-moh teh see-EHN-tehs

Do you have any recommendations?
¿Tienes alguna recomendación?
Tee-EH-nehs ahl-GOO-nah rreh-koh-mehn-dah-see-OHN

When did you first come to China?
¿Cuándo viniste a China por primera vez?
KWAHN-doh vee-NEES-teh ah CHEE-nah pohr pree-MEH-rah vehs

Were you born here?
¿Naciste aquí?
Nah-SEES-teh ah-KEE

Come join me for the rest of the vacation.
Ven conmigo por el resto de las vacaciones.
Vehn kohn-MEE-goh pohr ehl RREHS-toh deh lahs vah-kah-see-OH-nehs

What times do the shops open in this area?
¿A qué hora abren las tiendas en esta zona?
Ah keh OH-rah AH-brehn lahs tee-EHN-dahs ehn EHS-tah SOH-nah

Is there tax-free shopping available?
¿Hay tiendas libres de impuestos?
AH-ee tee-EHN-dahs LEE-brehs deh eem-PWEHS-tohs

Where can I change currency?
¿Dónde puedo cambiar de moneda?
DOHN-deh PWEH-doh kahm-bee-AHR deh moh-NEH-dah

Is it legal to drink in this area?
¿Es legal beber en esta área?
Ehs leh-GAHL beh-BEHR ehn EHS-tah AH-reh-ah

Can I smoke in this area?
¿Puedo fumar en esta área?
PWEH-doh foo-MAHR ehn EHS-tah AH-reh-ah

What about this?
¿Qué tal esto?
Keh tahl EHS-toh

Can I park here?
¿Puedo estacionar aquí?
PWEH-doh ehs-tah-see-oh-NAHR ah-KEE

Have you gotten used to living in Spain by now?
¿Ya te acostumbraste a vivir en España?
Yah teh ah-kohs-toom-BRAHS-teh ah vee-VEER ehn ehs-PAH-nyah

How much does it cost to park here?
¿Cuánto cuesta estacionar aquí?
KWAHN-toh KWEHS-tah ehs-tah-see-oh-NAHR ah-KEE

How long can I park here?
¿Por cuánto tiempo puedo estacionar aquí?
Pohr KWAHN-toh tee-EHM-poh PWEH-doh ehs-tah-see-oh-NAHR ah-KEE

Where can I get some directions?
¿Dónde pueden darme algunas direcciones?
DOHN-deh PWEH-dehn DAHR-meh ahl-GOO-nahs dee-rehk-see-OH-nehs

Can you point me in the direction of the bridge?
¿Puedes decirme hacia dónde está el puente?
PWEH-dehs deh-SEER-meh AH-see-ah DOHN-deh ehs-TAH ehl PWEHN-teh

What can I do here for fun?
¿Qué puedo hacer aquí para divertirme?
Keh PWEH-doh ah-SEHR ah-KEE PAH-rah dee-vehr-TEER-meh

Is this a family friendly place?
¿Este lugar es bueno para las familias?
EHS-teh loo-GAHR ehs BWEH-noh PAH-rah lahs fah-MEE-lee-ahs

Are kids allowed here?
¿Se permiten niños aquí?
Seh pehr-MEE-tehn NEE-nyohs ah-KEE

Where can I find the park?
¿Dónde puedo encontrar el parque?
DOHN-deh PWEH-doh ehn-kohn-TRAHR ehl PAHR-keh

How do I get back to my hotel?
¿Cómo puedo regresar a mi hotel?
KOH-moh PWEH-doh rreh-greh-SAHR ah mee oh-TEHL

Where can I get some medicine?
¿Dónde puedo conseguir algunas medicinas?
DOHN-deh PWEH-doh kohn-seh-GEER ahl-GOO-nahs meh-dee-SEE-nahs

Is my passport safe here?
¿Mi pasaporte está seguro aquí?
Mee pah-sah-POHR-teh ehs-TAH seh-GOO-roh ah-KEE

Do you have a safe for my passport and belongings?
¿Tienes una caja fuerte para guardar mi pasaporte y pertenencias?
Tee-EH-nehs OO-nah KAH-hah foo-EHR-teh PAH-rah goo-ahr-DAHR mee
pah-sah-POHR-teh ee pehr-teh-NEHN-see-ahs

Is it safe to be here past midnight?
¿Es seguro estar aquí después de la medianoche?
Ehs seh-GOO-roh ehs-TAHR ah-KEE dehs-PWEHS deh lah meh-dee-ah-
NOH-cheh

When is the best time to visit this shop?
¿Cuál es la mejor hora para visitar esta tienda?
Kwahl ehs lah meh-HOHR OH-rah PAH-rah vee-see-TAHR EHS-tah tee-
EHN-dah

What is the best hotel in the area?
¿Cuál es el mejor hotel de la zona?
Kwahl ehs ehl meh-HOHR oh-TEHL deh lah SOH-nah

What attractions are close to my hotel?
¿Qué atracciones están cerca de mi hotel?
Keh ah-trahk-see-OH-nehs ehs-TAHN SEHR-kah deh mee oh-TEHL

Do you have any advice for tourists?
¿Tienes algún consejo para los turistas?
Tee-EH-nehs ahl-GOON kohn-SEH-hoh PAH-rah lohs too-REES-tahs

Do you have a list of the top things to do in the area?
¿Tienes una lista de las mejores cosas que hacer en el área?
Tee-EH-nehs OO-nah LEES-tah deh lahs meh-HOH-rehs KOH-sahs keh ah-
SEHR ehn ehl AH-reh-ah

What do I need to pack to go there?
¿Qué cosas debo empacar para ir allí?
Keh KOH-sahs DEH-boh ehm-pah-KAHR PAH-rah eer ah-YEE

Can you recommend some good food to eat?
¿Puedes recomendarme alguna comida buena?
PWEH-dehs rreh-koh-mehn-DAHR-meh ahl-GOO-nah koh-MEE-dah BWEH-nah

What should I do with my time here?
¿Qué debería hacer mientras estoy aquí?
Keh deh-beh-REE-ah ah-SEHR mee-EHN-trahs ehs-TOH-ee ah-KEE

What is the cheapest way to get from my hotel to the shop?
¿Cuál es la forma más barata de ir de mi hotel a la tienda?
Kwahl ehs lah FOHR-mah mahs bah-RAH-tah deh eer deh mee oh-TEHL ah lah tee-EHN-dah

What do you think of my itinerary?
¿Qué piensas de mi itinerario?
Keh pee-EHN-sahs deh mee ee-tee-neh-RAH-ree-oh

Does my phone work in this country?
¿Mi teléfono funciona en este país?
Mee teh-LEH-foh-noh foon-see-OH-nah ehn EHS-teh pah-EES

What is the best route to get to my hotel?
¿Cuál es la mejor ruta para llegar a mi hotel?
Kwahl ehs lah meh-HOHR RROO-tah PAH-rah yeh-GAHR ah mee oh-TEHL

Will the weather be okay for outside activities?
¿El clima será bueno para las actividades en exteriores?
Ehl KLEE-mah seh-RAH BWEH-noh PAH-rah lahs ahk-tee-vee-DAH-dehs ehn ehks-teh-ree-OH-rehs

Was that rude?
¿Eso fue grosero?
EH-soh foo-EH groh-SEH-roh

Where should I stay away from?
¿De qué lugares debería alejarme?
Deh keh loo-GAH-rehs deh-beh-REE-ah ah-leh-HAHR-meh

What is the best dive site in the area?
¿Cuál es el mejor lugar para bucear en el área?
Kwahl ehs ehl meh-HOHR loo-GAHR PAH-rah boo-seh-AHR ehn ehl AH-reh-ah

What is the best beach in the area?
¿Cuál es la mejor playa del área?
Kwahl ehs lah meh-HOHR PLAH-yah dehl AH-reh-ah

Do I need reservations?
¿Necesito una reserva?
Neh-seh-SEE-toh OO-nah rreh-SEHR-vah

I need directions to the best local food.
Necesito indicaciones para la mejor comida local.
Neh-seh-SEE-toh een-dee-kah-see-OH-nehs PAH-rah lah meh-HOHR
koh-MEE-dah loh-KAHL

What's your name?
¿Cuál es tu nombre?
Kwahl ehs too NOHM-breh

Where is the nearest place to eat?
¿Cuál es el lugar más cercano para comer?
Kwahl ehs ehl loo-GAHR mahs sehr-KAH-noh PAH-rah koh-MEHR

Where is the nearest hotel?
¿Dónde está el hotel más cercano?
DOHN-deh ehs-TAH ehl oh-TEHL mahs sehr-KAH-noh

Where is transportation?
¿Dónde está el transporte?
DOHN-deh ehs-TAH ehl trahns-POHR-teh

How much is this?
¿Cuánto es esto?
KWAHN-toh ehs EHS-toh

Do you pay tax here?
¿Ustedes pagan impuestos aquí?
Oos-TEH-dehs PAH-gahn eem-PWEHS-tohs ah-KEE

What types of payment are accepted?
¿Qué medios de pago aceptan?
Keh MEH-dee-ohs deh PAH-goh ah-SEHP-tahn

Can you help me read this?
¿Puedes ayudarme a leer esto?
PWEH-dehs ah-yoo-DAHR-meh ah leh-EHR EHS-toh

What languages do you speak?
¿Qué idiomas hablas?
Keh ee-dee-OH-mahs AH-blahs

Is it difficult to speak English?
¿Es difícil hablar inglés?
Ehs dee-FEE-seel ah-BLAHR een-GLEHS

What does that mean?
¿Eso qué significa?
EH-soh keh seeg-nee-FEE-kah

What is your name?
¿Cuál es tu nombre?
Kwahl ehs too NOHM-breh

Do you have a lighter?
¿Tienes un encendedor?
Tee-EH-nehs oon ehn-sehn-deh-DOHR

Do you have a match?
¿Tienes un fósforo?
Tee-EH-nehs oon FOHS-foh-roh

Is this a souvenir from your country?
¿Este es un souvenir de tu país?
EHS-teh ehs oon soo-veh-NEER deh too pah-EES

What is this?
¿Qué es esto?
Keh ehs EHS-toh

Can I ask you a question?
¿Puedo hacerte una pregunta?
PWEH-doh ah-SEHR-teh OO-nah preh-GOON-tah

Where is the safest place to store my travel information?
¿Cuál es el lugar más seguro para guardar mi información de viaje?
Kwahl ehs ehl loo-GAHR mahs seh-GOO-roh PAH-rah goo-ahr-DAHR mee een-fohr-mah-see-OHN deh vee-AH-heh

Will you come along with me?
¿Vendrás conmigo?
Vehn-DRAHS kohn-MEE-goh

Is this your first time here?
¿Esta es tu primera vez aquí?
EHS-tah ehs too pree-MEH-rah vehs ah-KEE

What is your opinion on the matter?
¿Cuál es tu opinión al respecto?
Kwahl ehs too oh-pee-nee-OHN ahl rrehs-PEHK-toh

Will this spoil if I leave it out too long?
¿Esto se dañará si lo dejo afuera por mucho tiempo?
EHS-toh seh dah-nyah-RAH see loh DEH-hoh ah-foo-EH-rah pohr MOO-choh tee-EHM-poh

What side of the sidewalk do I walk on?
¿Por qué lado de la acera debo caminar?
Pohr keh LAH-doh deh lah ah-SEH-rah DEH-boh kah-mee-NAHR

What do those lights mean?
¿Qué significan esas luces?
Keh seeg-nee-FEE-kahn EH-sahs LOO-sehs

Can I walk up these stairs?
¿Puedo subir por estas escaleras?
PWEH-doh soo-BEER pohr EHS-tahs ehs-kah-LEH-rahs

Is that illegal here?
¿Eso es ilegal aquí?
EH-soh ehs ee-leh-GAHL ah-KEE

How much trouble would I get in if I did that?
¿En cuántos problemas me metería si hiciera eso?
Ehn KWAHN-tohs proh-BLEH-mahs meh meh-teh-REE-ah see ee-see-EH-rah EH-soh

Why don't we all go together?
¿Por qué no vamos todos juntos?
Pohr keh noh VAH-mohs TOH-dohs HOON-tohs

May I throw away waste here?
¿Puedo botar basura aquí?
PWEH-doh boh-TAHR bah-SOO-rah ah-KEE

Where is the recycle bin?
¿Dónde está la papelera de reciclaje?

DOHN-deh ehs-TAH lah pah-peh-LEH-rah deh rreh-see-KLAH-heh

WHEN SOMEONE IS BEING RUDE

Please, close your mouth while chewing that.
Por favor, cierra la boca mientras masticas eso.
Pohr fah-VOHR see-EH-rrah lah BOH-kah mee-EHN-trahs mahs-TEE-kahs EH-soh

Don't ask me again, please.
Por favor, no me vuelvas a preguntar.
Pohr fah-VOHR, noh meh voo-EHL-vahs ah preh-goon-TAHR

I'm not paying for that.
No voy a pagar por eso.
Noh VOH-ee ah pah-GAHR pohr EH-soh

Leave me alone or I am calling the authorities.
Aléjate de mí o llamo a las autoridades.
Ah-LEH-hah-teh deh mee oh YAH-moh ah lahs ah-oo-toh-ree-DAH-dehs

Hurry up!
¡Apúrate!
Ah-POO-rah-teh

Stop bothering me!
¡Deja de molestarme!
DEH-hah deh moh-lehs-TAHR-meh

Don't bother me, please!
¡Por favor, no me molestes!
Pohr fah-VOHR, noh meh moh-LEHS-tehs

Are you content?
¿Estás contento?
Ehs-TAHS kohn-TEHN-toh

I'm walking away, please don't follow me.
Me voy, no me sigas por favor.
Meh VOH-ee, noh meh SEE-gahs pohr fah-VOHR

You stole my shoes and I would like them back.
Robaste mis zapatos y los quiero de vuelta.
Rroh-BAHS-teh mees sah-PAH-tohs ee lohs kee-EH-roh deh voo-EHL-tah

You have the wrong person.
Te equivocaste de persona.
Teh eh-kee-voh-KAHS-teh deh pehr-SOH-nah

I think you are incorrect.
Creo que estás equivocado.
KREH-oh keh ehs-TAHS eh-kee-voh-KAH-doh

Stop waking me up!
¡Deja de despertarme!
DEH-hah deh dehs-pehr-TAHR-meh

You're talking too much.
Hablas demasiado.
AH-blahs deh-mah-see-AH-doh

That hurts!
¡Eso duele!
EH-soh doo-EH-leh

I need you to apologize.
Necesito que te disculpes.
Neh-seh-SEE-toh keh teh dees-KOOL-pehs

Stay away from my children!
¡Aléjate de mis hijos!
Ah-LEH-hah-teh deh mees EE-hohs

Don't touch me.
No me toques.
Noh meh TOH-kehs

I would appreciate it if you didn't take my seat.
Te agradecería que no tomaras mi asiento.
Teh ah-grah-deh-seh-REE-ah keh noh toh-MAH-rahs mee ah-see-EHN-toh

You didn't tell me that.
Tú no me dijiste eso.
Too noh meh dee-HEES-teh EH-soh

You are price gouging me.
Ese precio no es justo.
EH-seh PREH-see-oh noh ehs HOOS-toh

Please be quiet, I am trying to listen.
Por favor, haz silencio, estoy tratando de escuchar.
Pohr fah-VOHR, ahs see-LEHN-see-oh, ehs-TOH-ee trah-TAHN-doh deh
ehs-koo-CHAHR

Don't interrupt me while I am talking.
No me interrumpas mientras hablo.
Noh meh een-teh-RROOM-pahs mee-EHN-trahs AH-bloh

Don't sit on my car and stay away from it.
No te sientes en mi auto y aléjate de él.
Noh teh see-EHN-tehs ehn mee AH-oo-toh ee ah-LEH-hah-teh deh ehl

Get out of my car.
Sal de mi auto.
Sahl deh mee AH-oo-toh

Get away from me and leave me alone!
¡Aléjate de mí y déjame en paz!
Ah-LEH-hah-teh deh mee ee DEH-hah-meh ehn pahs

You're being rude.
Estás siendo grosero.
Ehs-TAHS see-EHN-doh groh-SEH-roh

Please don't curse around my children.
Por favor, no digas vulgaridades frente a mis hijos.
Pohr fah-VOHR noh DEE-gahs vool-gah-ree-DAH-dehs FREHN-teh ah
mees EE-hohs

Let go of me!
¡Déjame ir!
DEH-hah-meh eer

I'm not going to tell you again.
No te lo voy a repetir.
Noh teh loh VOH-ee ah rreh-peh-TEER

Don't yell at me.
No me grites.
Noh meh GREE-tehs

Please lower your voice.
Por favor, baja la voz.
Pohr fah-VOHR, BAH-hah lah vohs

What is the problem?
¿Cuál es el problema?
Kwahl ehs ehl proh-BLEH-mah

I would appreciate it if you didn't take pictures of me.
Te agradecería que no me tomaras fotos.
Teh ah-grah-deh-seh-REE-ah keh noh meh toh-MAH-rahs FOH-tohs

I am very disappointed in the way you are behaving.
Estoy muy decepcionado por tu comportamiento.
Ehs-TOH-ee MOO-ee deh-sehp-see-oh-NAH-doh pohr too kohm-pohr-tah-mee-EHN-toh

Watch where you are walking!
¡Mira por dónde caminas!
MEE-rah pohr DOHN-deh kah-MEE-nahs

He just bumped into me!
¡Él me acaba de tropezar!
Ehl meh ah-KAH-bah deh troh-peh-SAHR

MEDICAL

I would like to set up an appointment with my doctor.
Me gustaría pedir una cita con mi doctor.
Meh goos-tah-REE-ah peh-DEER OO-nah SEE-tah kohn mee dohk-TOHR

I am a new patient and need to fill out forms.
Soy un nuevo paciente y necesito llenar los formularios.
SOH-ee oon NWEH-voh pah-see-EHN-teh ee neh-seh-SEE-toh yeh-NAHR
lohs fohr-moo-LAH-ree-ohs

I am allergic to certain medications.
Soy alérgico a ciertos medicamentos.
SOH-ee ah-LEHR-hee-koh ah see-EHR-tohs meh-dee-kah-MEHN-tohs

That is where it hurts.
Allí es donde me duele.
Ah-YEE ehs DOHN-deh meh doo-EH-leh

I have had the flu for three weeks.
He estado resfriado por tres semanas.
Eh ehs-TAH-do rrehs-free-AH-doh pohr trehs seh-MAH-nahs

It hurts when I walk on that foot.
Me duele caminar con ese pie.
Meh doo-EH-leh kah-mee-NAHR kohn EHS-teh pee-EH

When is my next appointment?
¿Cuándo es mi próxima cita?
KWAHN-doh ehs mee PROHK-see-mah SEE-tah

Does my insurance cover this?
¿Esto lo cubre mi seguro?
EHS-toh loh KOO-breh mee seh-GOO-roh

Do you want to take a look at my throat?
¿Quiere ver mi garganta?
Kee-EH-reh vehr mee gahr-GAHN-tah

Do I need to fast before going there?
¿Tengo que ayunar antes de ir allí?
TEHN-goh keh ah-yoo-NAHR an-TEHS deh ihr Ah-llee

Is there a generic version of this medicine?
¿Hay una versión genérica de este medicamento?
AH-ee OO-nah vehr-see-OHN heh-NEH-ree-kah deh EHS-teh meh-dee-kah-MEHN-toh

I need to get back on dialysis.
Necesito diálisis de nuevo.
Neh-seh-SEE-toh dee-AH-lee-sees deh NWEH-voh

My blood type is A.
Mi tipo de sangre es A.
Mee TEE-poh deh SAHN-greh ehs ah

I will be more than happy to donate blood.
Estaré más que feliz de donar sangre.
Ehs-tah-REH mahs keh feh-LEES deh doh-NAHR SAHN-greh

I have been feeling dizzy.
Me he sentido mareado.
Meh eh sehn-TEE-doh mah-reh-AH-doh

The condition is getting worse.
La condición está empeorando.
Lah kohn-dee-see-OHN ehs-TAH ehm-peh-oh-RAHN-doh

The medicine has made the condition a little better, but it is still there.
La medicina me ha mejorado un poco, pero la condición sigue ahí.
Lah meh-dee-SEE-nah meh ah meh-hoh-RAH-doh oon POH-koh, peh-roh lah kohn-dee-see-OHN SEE-geh ah-EE

Is my initial health examination tomorrow?
¿Mi examen de salud inicial es mañana?
Mee ehk-SAH-mehn deh sah-LOOD ee-nee-see-AHL ehs mah-NYAH-nah

I would like to switch doctors.
Me gustaría cambiar de doctor.
Meh goos-tah-REE-ah kahm-bee-AHR deh dohk-TOHR

Can you check my blood pressure?
¿Puedes revisar mi presión sanguínea?
PWEH-dehs rreh-vee-SAHR mee preh-see-OHN sahn-GEE-neh-ah

I have a fever that won't go away.
Tengo una fiebre que no se va.
TEHN-goh OO-nah fee-EH-breh keh noh seh vah

I think my arm is broken.
Creo que me fracturé el brazo.
KREH-oh keh meh frahk-too-REH ehl BRAH-soh

I think I have a concussion.
Creo que tengo una contusión.
KREH-oh keh TEHN-goh OO-nah kohn-too-see-OHN

My eyes refuse to focus.
No puedo enfocar la vista.
Noh PWEH-doh ehn-foh-KAHR lah VEES-tah

I have double vision.
Veo doble.
VEH-oh DOH-bleh

Is surgery the only way to fix this?
¿La cirugía es la única opción?
Lah see-roo-HEE-ah ehs lah OO-nee-kah ohp-see-OHN

Who are you referring me to?
¿A quién me está refiriendo?
Ah kee-EHN meh ehs-TAH rreh-fee-ree-EHN-doh

Where is the waiting room?
¿Dónde está la sala de espera?
DOHN-deh ehs-TAH lah SAH-lah deh ehs-PEH-rah

Can I bring someone with me into the office?
¿Puedo entrar al consultorio con alguien?
PWEH-doh ehn-TRAHR ahl kohn-sool-TOH-ree-oh kohn AHL-gee-ehn

I need help filling out these forms.
Necesito ayuda para llenar estos formularios.
Neh-seh-SEE-toh ah-YOO-dah PAH-rah yeh-NAHR EHS-tohs fohr-moo-LAH-ree-ohs

Do you take Cobra as an insurance provider?
¿Aceptan a Cobra como compañía de seguros?
Ah-SEHP-tahn ah KOH-brah KOH-moh kohm-pah-NYEE-ah deh seh-GOO-rohs

What is my copayment?
¿Cuánto es mi copago?
KWAHN-toh ehs mee koh-PAH-goh

What forms of payment do you accept?
¿Qué métodos de pago aceptan?
Keh MEH-toh-dohs deh PAH-goh ah-SEHP-tahn

Do you have a payment plan or is it all due now?
¿Tienen plan de financiación o el pago vence ya?
Tee-EH-nehn plahn deh fee-nahn-see-ah-see-OHN oh ehl PAH-goh
VEHN-seh yah

My old doctor prescribed something different.
Mi antiguo doctor me recetó algo diferente.
Mee ahn-TEE-goo-oh dohk-TOHR meh rreh-seh-TOH AHL-goh dee-feh-
REHN-teh

Will you take a look at my leg?
¿Revisará mi pierna?
Rreh-vee-sah-RAH mee pee-EHR-nah

I need to be referred to a gynecologist.
Necesito que me remita a un ginecólogo.
Neh-seh-SEE-toh keh meh rreh-MEE-tah ah oon hee-neh-KOH-loh-goh

I am unhappy with the medicine you prescribed me.
No estoy satisfecho con la medicina que me recetó.
Noh ehs-TOH-ee sah-tees-FEH-choh kohn lah meh-dee-SEE-nah keh meh
rreh-seh-TOH

Do you see patients on the weekend?
¿Atiende los fines de semana?
Ah-tee-EHN-deh lohs FEE-nehs deh seh-MAH-nah

I need a good therapist.
Necesito un buen terapeuta.
Neh-seh-SEE-toh oon bwehn teh-rah-PEH-oo-tah

How long will it take me to rehab this injury?
¿Cuánto tiempo me tomará recuperarme de esta herida?
KWAHN-toh tee-EHM-poh meh toh-mah-RAH rreh-koo-peh-RAHR-meh
deh EHS-tah eh-REE-dah

I have not gone to the bathroom in over a week.
No he ido al baño en más de una semana.
Noh eh EE-doh ahl BAH-nyoh ehn mahs deh OO-nah seh-MAH-nah

I am constipated and feel bloated.
Estoy estreñido y me siento hinchado.
Ehs-TOH-ee ehs-treh-NYEE-doh ee meh see-EHN-toh een-CHAH-doh

It hurts when I go to the bathroom.
Me duele ir al baño.
Meh doo-EH-leh eer ahl BAH-nyoh

I have not slept well at all since getting here.
No he dormido bien desde que estoy aquí.
Noh eh dohr-MEE-doh bee-EHN DEHS-deh keh ehs-TOH-ee ah-KEE

Do you have any pain killers?
¿Tienes algún analgésico?
Tee-EH-nehs ahl-GOON ah-nahl-HEH-see-koh

I am allergic to that medicine.
Soy alérgico a ese medicamento.
SOH-ee ah-LEHR-hee-koh ah EH-seh meh-dee-kah-MEHN-toh

How long will I be under observation?
¿Por cuánto tiempo estaré bajo observación?
Pohr KWAHN-toh tee-EHM-poh ehs-tah-REH BAH-hoh ohb-sehr-vah-see-OHN

I have a toothache.
Tengo dolor de muela.
TEHN-goh doh-LOHR deh moo-EH-lah

Do I need to see a dentist?
¿Necesito ver a un dentista?
Neh-seh-SEE-toh vehr ah oon dehn-TEES-tah

Does my insurance cover dental?
¿Mi seguro cubre servicios dentales?
Mee seh-GOO-roh KOO-breh sehr-VEE-see-ohs dehn-TAH-lehs

My diarrhea won't go away.
Mi diarrea no se va.
Mee dee-ah-RREH-ah noh seh vah

Can I have a copy of the receipt for my insurance?
¿Puedes darme una copia de la factura para mi seguro?
PWEH-dehs DAHR-meh OO-nah KOH-pee-ah deh lah fahk-TOO-rah PAH-rah mee seh-GOO-roh

I need a pregnancy test.
Necesito una prueba de embarazo.
Neh-seh-SEE-toh OO-nah proo-EH-bah deh ehm-bah-RAH-soh

I think I may be pregnant.
Creo que puedo estar embarazada.
KREH-oh keh PWEH-doh ehs-TAHR ehm-bah-rah-SAH-dah

Can we please see a pediatrician?
¿Podemos ver a un pediatra, por favor?
Poh-DEH-mohs vehr ah oon peh-dee-AH-trah, pohr FAH-vohr

I have had trouble breathing.
He tenido problemas respiratorios.
Eh teh-NEE-doh proh-BLEH-mahs rrehs-pee-rah-TOH-ree-ohs

My sinuses are acting up.
Mi sinusitis está muy activa.
Mee see-noo-SEE-tees ehs-TAH MOO-ee ahk-TEE-vah

Will I still be able to breastfeed?
¿Aún podré amamantar?
Ah-OON poh-DREH ah-mah-mahn-TAHR

How long do I have to stay in bed?
¿Cuánto tiempo debo estar en cama?
KWAHN-toh tee-EHM-poh DEH-boh ehs-TAHR ehn KAH-mah

How long do I have to stay under hospital care?
¿Cuánto tiempo debo permanecer bajo atención hospitalaria?
KWAHN-toh tee-EHM-poh DEH-boh pehr-mah-neh-SEHR BAH-hoh ah-tehn-see-OHN ohs-pee-tah-LAH-ree-ah

Is it contagious?
¿Es contagioso?
Ehs kohn-tah-hee-OH-soh

How far along am I?
¿Qué tan avanzada estoy?
Keh tahn ah-vahn-SAH-dah ehs-TOH-ee

What did the x-ray say?
¿Qué mostró la radiografía?
Keh mohs-TROH lah rrah-dee-oh-grah-FEE-ah

Can I walk without a cane?
¿Puedo caminar sin bastón?
PWEH-doh kah-mee-NAHR seen bahs-TOHN

Is the wheelchair necessary?
¿La silla de ruedas es necesaria?
Lah SEE-yah deh roo-EH-dahs ehs neh-seh-SAH-ree-ah

Am I in the right area of the hospital?
¿Estoy en el área correcta del hospital?
Ehs-TOH-ee ehn ehl AH-reh-ah koh-RREHK-tah dehl ohs-pee-TAHL

Where is the front desk receptionist?
¿Dónde está la recepcionista?
DOHN-deh ehs-TAH lah rreh-sehp-see-oh-NEES-tah

I would like to go to a different waiting area.
Me gustaría ir a otra sala de espera.
Meh goos-tah-REE-ah eer ah OH-trah SAH-lah deh ehs-PEH-rah

Can I have a change of sheets please?
¿Puedes cambiar mis sábanas, por favor?
PWEH-dehs kahm-bee-AHR mees SAH-bah-nahs pohr fah-VOHR

Excuse me nurse, what is your name?
Disculpe, enfermera, ¿cuál es su nombre?
Dees-KOOL-peh, ehn-fehr-MEH-rah, kwahl ehs soo NOHM-breh

Who is the doctor in charge here?
¿Quién es el doctor a cargo aquí?
Kee-EHN ehs ehl dohk-TOHR ah KAHR-goh ah-KEE

I need some assistance, please.
Necesito ayuda, por favor.
Neh-seh-SEE-toh ah-YOO-da, pohr fah-VOHR

Will my recovery affect my ability to do work?
¿Mi recuperación afectará mi capacidad de trabajar?
Mee rreh-koo-peh-rah-see-OHN ah-fehk-tah-RAH mee kah-pah-see-DAHD deh trah-bah-HAHR

How long is the estimated recovery time?
¿Cuánto es el tiempo de recuperación estimado?
KWAHN-toh ehs ehl tee-EHM-poh deh rreh-koo-peh-rah-see-OHN ehs-tee-MAH-doh

Is that all you can do for me? There has to be another option.
¿Eso es todo lo que puedes hacer por mí? Tiene que haber otra opción.
EH-soh ehs TOH-doh loh keh PWEH-dehs ah-SEHR pohr mee. Tee-EH-neh keh ah-BEHR OH-trah ohp-see-OHN

I need help with motion sickness.
Necesito ayuda, tengo mareo.
Neh-seh-SEE-toh ah-YOO-dah, TEHN-goh mah-REH-oh

I'm afraid of needles.
Les tengo miedo a las agujas.
Lehs TEHN-goh mee-EH-doh ah lahs ah-GOO-hahs

My gown is too small, I need another one.
Mi bata es muy pequeña, necesito otra.
Mee BAH-tah ehs MOO-ee peh-KEH-nyah neh-seh-SEE-toh OH-trah

Can I have extra pillows?
¿Puedo tener más almohadas?
PWEH-doh teh-NEHR mahs ahl-moh-AH-dahs

I need assistance getting to the bathroom.
Necesito ayuda para llegar al baño.
Neh-seh-SEE-toh ah-YOO-dah PAH-rah yeh-GAHR ahl BAH-nyoh

Hi, is the doctor in?
Buenas, ¿está el doctor?
BWEH-nahs, ehs-TAH ehl dohk-TOHR

When should I schedule the next checkup?
¿Cuándo debo volver para la próxima cita de control?
KWAHN-doh DEH-boh vohl-VEHR PAH-rah lah PROHK-see-mah SEE-tah deh kohn-TROHL

When can I have these stitches removed?
¿Cuándo me pueden remover estos puntos?
KWAHN-doh meh PWEH-dehn rreh-moh-VEHR EHS-tohs POON-tohs

Do you have any special instructions while I'm in this condition?

¿Tienes instrucciones especiales para mi condición?

Tee-EH-nehs eens-trook-see-OH-nehs ehs-peh-see-AH-lehs PAH-rah mee kohn-dee-see-OHN

ORDERING FOOD

Can I see the menu?
¿Puedo ver el menú?
PWEH-doh vehr ehl meh-NOO

I'm really hungry. We should eat something soon.
Tengo mucha hambre. Deberíamos comer algo pronto.
TEHN-goh MOO-chah AHM-breh. Deh-beh-REE-ah-mohs koh-MEHR AHL-goh PROHN-toh

Can I take a look in the kitchen?
¿Puedo ver la cocina?
PWEH-doh vehr lah koh-SEE-nah

Can we see the drink menu?
¿Podemos ver el menú de bebidas?
Poh-DEH-mohs vehr ehl meh-NOO deh beh-BEE-dahs

When can we be seated?
¿Cuándo nos podemos sentar?
CU-ahn-do nohs poh-DEH-mohs sehn-TAHR

This is very tender and delicious.
Esto está muy tierno y delicioso.
EHS-toh ehs-TAH MOO-ee tee-EHR-noh ee deh-lee-see-OH-soh

Do you serve alcohol?
¿Tienes alcohol?
Tee-EH-nehs ahl-koh-OHL

I'm afraid our party can't make it.
Temo que nuestros invitados no vendrán
TEH-moh keh noo-ehs-trohs- een-vee-tah-dohs no vehn-drahn

That room is reserved for us.
Ese salón está reservado para nosotros.
EH-seh sah-LOHN ehs-TAH rreh-sehr-VAH-doh PAH-rah noh-SOH-trohs

Are there any seasonal favorites that you serve?
¿Tienes algunos platos favoritos de temporada?
Tee-EH-nehs ahl-GOO-nohs PLAH-tohs fah-voh-REE-tohs deh tehm-poh-RAH-dah

Do you offer discounts for kids or seniors?
¿Ofreces descuentos para niños o jubilados?
Oh-FREH-sehs dehs-koo-EHN-tohs PAH-rah NEE-nyohs oh hoo-bee-LAH-dohs

I would like it filleted.
Me gustaría fileteado.
Meh goos-tah-REE-ah fee-leh-teh-AH-doh

I would like to reserve a table for a party of four.
Me gustaría reservar una mesa para cuatro personas.
Meh goos-tah-REE-ah rreh-sehr-VAHR OO-nah MEH-sah PAH-rah KWAH-troh pehr-SOH-nahs

I would like to place the reservation under my name.
Me gustaría hacer una reserva a mi nombre.
Meh goos-tah-REE-ah ah-SEHR OO-nah rreh-SEHR-vah ah mee NOHM-breh

What type of alcohol do you serve?
¿Qué tipo de alcohol sirven?
Keh TEE-poh deh ahl-koh-OHL SEER-vehn

Do I need a reservation?
¿Necesito una reservación?
Neh-seh-SEE-toh OO-nah rreh-sehr-vah-see-OHN

What does it come with?
¿Con qué viene?
Kohn keh vee-EH-neh

What are the ingredients?
¿Cuáles son los ingredientes?
KWAH-lehs sohn lohs een-greh-dee-EHN-tehs

What else does the chef put in the dish?
¿Qué más pone el chef en el plato?
Keh mahs POH-neh ehl chehf ehn ehl PLAH-toh

I wonder which of these tastes better?
Me pregunto cuál de estos sabe mejor.
Meh preh-GOON-toh kwahl deh EHS-tohs SAH-beh meh-HOHR

That is incorrect. Our reservation was at noon.
Eso es incorrecto. Nuestra reservación era en la tarde.
EH-soh ehs een-koh-RREHK-toh. NWEHS-trah rreh-sehr-vah-see-OHN
EH-rah ehn lah TAHR-deh

I would like red wine please.
Yo quiero vino tinto, por favor.
Yoh kee-EH-roh VEE-noh TEEN-toh pohr fah-VOHR

Can you take the head for the soup?
¿Puedes guardar la cabeza para una sopa?
PWEH-dehs goo-ahr-DAHR lah kah-BEH-sah PAH-rah OO-nah SOH-pah

What is the most popular dish here?
¿Cuál es el plato más popular de aquí?
Kwahl ehs ehl PLAH-toh mahs poh-poo-LAHR deh ah-KEE

What are the specials today?
¿Cuáles son los especiales del día?
KWAH-lehs sohn lohs ehs-peh-see-AH-lehs dehl DEE-ah

What are your appetizers?
¿Cuáles son los aperitivos?
KWAH-lehs sohn lohs ah-peh-ree-TEE-vohs

Please bring these out separately.
Por favor, tráigalos por separado.
Pohr fah-VOHR, TRAH-ee-gah-lohs pohr seh-pah-RAH-doh

Do we leave a tip?
¿Dejamos propina?
Deh-HAH-mohs proh-PEE-nah

Are tips included with the bill?
¿Las propinas están incluidas en la cuenta?
Lahs proh-PEE-nahs ehs-TAHN een-kloo-EE-dahs ehn lah koo-EHN-tah

Split the bill, please.
Por favor, divide la cuenta.
Pohr fah-VOHR, dee-VEE-deh lah koo-EHN-tah

We are ordering separately.
Pediremos órdenes separadas.
Peh-dee-REH-mohs OHR-deh-nehs seh-pah-RAH-dahs

Is there an extra fee for sharing an entrée?
¿Hay una tarifa adicional por compartir una entrada?
AH-ee OO-nah tah-REE-fah ah-dee-see-oh-NAHL pohr kohm-pahr-TEER OO-nah ehn-TRAH-dah

Is there a local specialty that you recommend?
¿Hay alguna especialidad local que recomiendes?
AH-ee ahl-GOO-nah ehs-peh-see-ah-lee-DAHD loh-KAHL keh rreh-koh-mee-EHN-dehs

This looks different from what I originally ordered.
Esto no parece lo que yo pedí.
EHS-toh noh pah-REH-seh loh keh yoh peh-DEE

Is this a self-serve buffet?
¿Este es un buffet de autoservicio?
EHS-teh ehs oon boo-FEHT deh ah-oo-toh-sehr-VEE-see-oh

I want a different waiter.
Quiero a otro mesero.
Kee-EH-roh ah OH-troh meh-SEH-roh

Please move us to a different table.
Por favor, cámbianos a otra mesa.
Pohr fah-VOHR, KAHM-bee-ah-nohs ah OH-trah MEH-sah

Can we put two tables together?
¿Podemos juntar dos mesas?
Poh-DEH-mohs hoon-TAHR dohs MEH-sahs

My spoon is dirty. Can I have another one?
Mi cuchara está sucia, ¿puedes darme otra?
Mee koo-CHAH-rah ehs-TAH SOO-see-ah, PWEH-dehs DAHR-meh OH-trah

We need more napkins, please.
Necesitamos más servilletas, por favor.
Neh-seh-see-TAH-mohs mahs sehr-vee-YEH-tahs, pohr fah-VOHR

I'm a vegetarian and don't eat meat.
Soy vegetariano y no como carne.
SOH-ee veh-heh-tah-ree-AH-noh ee noh KOH-moh KAHR-neh

The table next to us is being too loud. Can you say something?
En la mesa de al lado hacen mucho ruido. ¿Puedes decirles algo?
Ehn lah MEH-sah deh ahl LAH-doh AH-sehn MOO-choh roo-EE-doh.
PWEH-dehs deh-SEER-lehs AHL-goh

Someone is smoking in our non smoking section.
Alguien está fumando en nuestra sección libre de humo.
AHL-gee-ehn ehs-TAH foo-MAHN-doh ehn NWEHS-trah sehk-see-OHN
LEE-breh deh OO-moh

Please seat us in a booth.
Ubícanos en una cabina, por favor.
Oo-BEE-kah-nohs ehn OO-nah kah-BEE-nah, pohr fah-VOHR

Do you have any nonalcoholic beverages?
¿Tienes bebidas no alcohólicas?
Tee-EH-nehs beh-BEE-dahs noh ahl-koh-OH-lee-kahs

Where is your bathroom?
¿Dónde está el baño?
DOHN-deh ehs-TAH ehl BAH-nyoh

Are you ready to order?
¿Están listos para ordenar?
Ehs-TAHN LEES-tohs PAH-rah ohr-deh-NAHR

Five more minutes, please.
Cinco minutos más, por favor.
SEEN-koh mee-NOO-tohs mahs, pohr fah-VOHR

What time do you close?
¿A qué hora cierran?
Ah keh OH-rah see-EH-rrahn

Is there pork in this dish? I don't eat pork.
¿Este plato trae cerdo? No como cerdo.
EHS-teh PLAH-toh TRAH-eh SEHR-doh. Noh KOH-moh SEHR-doh

Do you have any dishes for vegans?
¿Tienes platos para veganos?
Tee-EH-nehs PLAH-tohs PAH-rah veh-GAH-nohs

Are these vegetables fresh?
¿Estos vegetales están frescos?
EHS-tohs veh-heh-TAH-lehs ehs-TAHN FREHS-kohs

Have any of these vegetables been cooked in butter?
¿Alguno de estos vegetales ha sido cocinado con mantequilla?
Ahl-GOO-noh deh EHS-tohs veh-heh-TAH-lehs ah SEE-doh koh-see-NAH-doh kohn mahn-teh-KEE-yah

Is this spicy?
¿Esto es picante?
EHS-toh ehs pee-KAHN-teh

Is this sweet?
¿Esto es dulce?
EHS-toh ehs DOOL-seh

I want more please.
Quiero más, por favor.
Kee-EH-roh mahs, pohr fah-VOHR

I would like a dish containing these items.
Quiero un plato con estos ingredientes.
Kee-EH-roh oon PLAH-toh kohn EHS-tohs een-greh-dee-EHN-tehs

Can you make this dish light? Thank you.
¿Puedes hacer este plato más ligero? Gracias.
PWEH-dehs ah-SEHR EHS-teh PLAH-toh mahs lee-HEH-roh. GRAH-see-ahs

Nothing else.
Nada más.
NAH-dah mahs

Please clear the plates.
Por favor, retira los platos.
Pohr fah-VOHR, rreh-TEE-rah lohs PLAH-tohs

May I have a cup of soup?
¿Puedes traerme un plato de sopa?
PWEH-dehs trah-EHR-meh oon PLAH-toh deh SOH-pah

Do you have any bar snacks?
¿Tienes aperitivos?
Tee-EH-nehs ah-peh-ree-TEE-vohs

Another round, please.
Otra ronda, por favor.
OH-trah RROHN-dah, pohr fah-VOHR

When is closing time for the bar?
¿A qué hora cierra el bar?
Ah keh OH-rah see-EH-rrah ehl bahr

That was delicious!
¡Estuvo delicioso!
Ehs-TOO-voh deh-lee-see-OH-soh

Does this have alcohol in it?
¿Esto tiene alcohol?
EHS-toh tee-EH-neh ahl-koh-OHL

Does this have nuts in it?
¿Este plato tiene nueces?
EHS-teh PLAH-toh tee-EH-neh NWEH-sehs

Is this gluten free?
¿Este plato es libre de gluten?
EHS-teh PLAH-toh ehs LEE-breh deh GLOO-tehn

Can I get this to go?
¿Puedes darme esto para llevar?
PWEH-dehs DAHR-meh EHS-toh PAH-rah yeh-VAHR

May I have a refill?
¿Puedo recargar?
PWEH-doh rreh-kahr-GAHR

Is this dish kosher?
¿Este plato es kósher?
EHS-teh PLAH-toh ehs kosher

I would like to change my drink.
Quisiera cambiar mi bebida.
Kee-see-EH-rah kahm-bee-AHR mee beh-BEE-dah

My coffee is cold. Could you please warm it up?
Mi café está frío. ¿Podrías calentarlo, por favor?
Mee kah-FEH ehs-TAH FREE-oh. Poh-DREE-ahs kah-lehn-TAHR-loh, pohr fah-VOHR

Do you serve coffee?
¿Tienen café?
Tee-EH-nehn kah-FEH

Can I please have cream in my coffee?
¿Puedes ponerle crema a mi café, por favor?
PWEH-dehs poh-NEHR-leh KREH-mah ah mee kah-FEH, pohr fah-VOHR

Please add extra sugar to my coffee.
Por favor, ponle azúcar extra a mi café.
Pohr fah-VOHR, POHN-leh ah-SOO-kahr EKS-trah ah mee kah-FEH

I would like to have my coffee served black, no cream and no sugar.
Quisiera que mi café sea negro, sin azúcar o crema.
Kee-see-EH-rah keh mee kah-FEH SEH-ah NEH-groh, seen ah-SOO-kahr oh KREH-mah

I would like to have decaffeinated coffee, please.
Quisiera café descafeinado, por favor.
Kee-see-EH-rah kah-FEH dehs-kah-feh-ee-NAH-doh, pohr fah-VOHR

Do you serve coffee flavored ice cream?
¿Tienen helado de café?
Tee-EH-nehn eh-LAH-doh deh kah-FEH

Please put my cream and sugar on the side so that I can add it myself.
Por favor, pon el azúcar y la crema aparte para servirlos yo mismo.
Pohr fah-VOHR, pohn ehl ah-SOO-kahr ee lah KREH-mah ah-PAHR-teh PAH-rah sehr-VEER-lohs yoh mees-moh

I would like to order an iced coffee.
Quisiera ordenar un café helado.
Kee-see-EH-rah ohr-deh-NAHR oon kah-FEH eh-LAH-doh.

I would like an Espresso please.
Quisiera un café expreso, por favor.
Kee-see-EH-rah oon kah-FEH ehks-PREH-soh, pohr fah-VOHR

Do you have 2% milk?
¿Tienes leche al 2%?
Tee-EH-nehs LEH-cheh ahl dohs pohr see-EHN-toh

Do you serve soy milk?
¿Tienes leche de soya?
Tee-EH-nehs LEH-cheh deh SOH-yah

Do you have almond milk?
¿Tienes leche de almendras?
Tee-EH-nehs LEH-cheh deh ahl-MEHN-drahs

Are there any alternatives to the milk you serve?
¿Tienes otro tipo de leche?
Tee-EH-nehs OH-troh TEE-poh deh LEH-cheh

Please put the lemons for my tea on the side.
Por favor, pon los limones aparte del té.
Pohr fah-VOHR, pohn lohs lee-MOH-nehs ah-PAHR-teh dehl teh

No lemons with my tea, thank you.
Mi té sin limones, gracias.
Mee teh seen lee-MOH-nehs, GRAH-see-ahs

Is your water from the tap?
¿Su agua es de grifo?
Soo AH-wah ehs deh GREE-foh

Sparkling water, please.
Agua con gas, por favor.
AH-wah kohn gahs, pohr fah-VOHR

Can I get a diet coke?
¿Puedes darme una Coca-Cola de dieta
PWEH-dehs DAHR-meh OO-nah Coca-Cola deh dee-eh-TAH

We're ready to order.
Estamos listos para ordenar.
Ehs-TAH-mohs LEES-tohs PAH-rah ohr-deh-NAHR

Can we be seated over there instead?
¿Podemos sentarnos allá mejor?
Poh-DEH-mohs sehn-TAHR-nohs ah-YAH meh-HOHR

Can we have a seat outside?
¿Puedes ubicarnos afuera?
PWEH-dehs oo-bee-KAHR-nohs ah-foo-EH-rah

Please hold the salt.
Por favor, ten la sal.
Pohr fah-VOHR, tehn lah sahl

This is what I would like for my main course.
Me gustaría esto para mi plato principal.
Meh goos-tah-REE-ah EHS-toh PAH-rah mee PLAH-toh preen-see-PAHL

I would like the soup instead of the salad.
Prefiero la sopa en vez de la ensalada.
Preh-fee-EH-roh lah SOH-pah ehn vehs deh lah ehn-sah-LAH-dah

I'll have the chicken risotto.
Yo quiero el risotto de pollo.
Yoh kee-EH-roh ehl ree-SOH-toh deh POH-yoh

Can I change my order?
¿Puedo cambiar mi orden?
PWEH-doh kahm-bee-AHR mee OHR-dehn

Do you have a kid's menu?
¿Tienen menú infantil?
Tee-EH-nehn meh-NOO een-fahn-TEEL

When does the lunch menu end?
¿A qué hora termina el menú del almuerzo?
Ah keh OH-rah tehr-MEE-nah ehl meh-NOO dehl ahl-moo-EHR-soh

When does the dinner menu start?
¿A qué hora comienza el menú de la cena?
Ah keh OH-rah koh-mee-EHN-sah ehl meh-NOO deh lah SEH-nah

Do you have any recommendations from the menu?
¿Me recomiendas algo del menú?
Meh rreh-koh-mee-EHN-dahs AHL-goh dehl meh-NOO

I would like to place an off-menu order.
Quisiera pedir algo que no está en el menú.
Kee-see-EH-rah peh-DEER AHL-goh keh noh ehs-TAH ehn ehl meh-NOO

Can we see the dessert menu?
¿Puedes traernos el menú de postres?
PWEH-dehs trah-EHR-nohs ehl meh-NOO deh POHS-trehs

Is this available sugar free?
¿Tienes esto sin azúcar?
Tee-EH-nehs EHS-toh seen ah-SOO-kahr

May we have the bill, please?
Puedes darnos la cuenta, por favor.
PWEH-dehs DAHR-nohs lah koo-EHN-tah, pohr fah-VOHR

Where do we pay?
¿Dónde pagamos?
DOHN-deh pah-GAH-mohs

Hi, we are for the party of Isaac.
Hola, estamos aquí para la fiesta de Isaac.
OH-lah, ehs-TAH-mohs ah-KEE PAH-rah lah fee-EHS-tah deh ee-sah-AHK

We haven't made up our minds yet on what to order. Can we have a few more minutes, please?
Aún no hemos decidido qué ordenar. ¿Puedes darnos unos minutos más, por favor?
Ah-OON noh EH-mohs deh-see-DEE-doh keh ohr-deh-NAHR. PWEH-dehs DAHR-nohs OO-nohs mee-NOO-tohs mahs, pohr fah-VOHR

Waiter!
¡Mesero!
Meh-SEH-roh

Waitress!
¡Mesera!
Meh-SEH-rah

I'm still deciding, come back to me, please.
Aún estoy decidiendo. Vuelve en un rato, por favor.
Ah-OON ehs-TOH-ee deh-see-dee-EHN-doh. Voo-EHL-veh ehn oon RRAH-toh, pohr fah-VOHR

Can we have a pitcher of that?
¿Puedes traernos una jarra de eso?
PWEH-dehs trah-EHR-nohs OO-nah HAH-rrah deh EH-oh

This is someone else's meal.
Esta es la orden de otra persona.
EHS-tah ehs lah OHR-dehn deh OH-trah pehr-SOH-nah

Can you please heat this up a little more?
¿Puedes calentar esto un poco más, por favor?
PWEH-dehs kah-lehn-TAHR EHS-toh oon POH-koh mahs, pohr fah-VOHR

I'm afraid I didn't order this.
Me temo que yo no ordené esto.
Meh TEH-moh keh yoh noh ohr-deh-NEH EHS-toh

Same again, please.
Otro igual, por favor.
OH-troh ee-goo-AHL, pohr fah-VOHR

Can we have another bottle of wine?
¿Puedes darnos otra botella de vino?
PWEH-dehs DAHR-nohs OH-trah boh-TEH-yah deh VEE-noh

That was perfect, thank you!
¡Perfecto, gracias!
Pehr-FEHK-toh, GRAH-see-ahs

Everything was good.
Todo estuvo muy bien.
TOH-doh ehs-TOO-voh MOO-ee bee-EHN

Can we have the bill?
¿Puedes darnos la cuenta?
PWEH-dehs DAHR-nohs lah koo-EHN-tah

I'm sorry, but this bill is incorrect.
Disculpa, la factura es incorrecta.
Dees-KOOL-pah, lah fahk-TOO-rah ehs een-koh-RREHK-tah

Can I have clean cutlery?
¿Puedes darme cubiertos limpios?
PWEH-dehs DAHR-meh koo-bee-EHR-tohs LEEM-pee-ohs

Can we have more napkins?
¿Puedes darnos más servilletas?
PWEH-dehs DAHR-nohs mahs sehr-vee-YEH-tahs

May I have another straw?
¿Puedes darme otra pajilla?

PWEH-dehs DAHR-meh OH-trah pah-HEE-yah

What sides can I have with that?
¿Qué acompañantes vienen con eso?
Keh ah-kohm-pah-NYAHN-tehs vee-EH-nehn kohn EH-so

Excuse me, but this is overcooked.
Disculpa, mi comida está quemada.
Dees-KOOL-pah, mee koh-MEE-dah ehs-TAH keh-MAH-dah

May I talk to the chef?
¿Puedo hablar con el chef?
PWEH-doh ah-BLAHR kohn ehl chehf

We have booked a table for fifteen people.
Reservamos una mesa para quince personas.
Rreh-sehr-VAH-mohs OO-nah MEH-sah PAH-rah KEEN-seh pehr-SOH-nahs

Are there any tables free?
¿Hay mesas disponibles?
AH-ee MEH-sahs des-poh-NEE-blehs

I would like one beer, please.
Quisiera una cerveza, por favor.
Kee-see-EH-rah OO-nah sehr-VEH-sah, pohr fah-VOHR

Can you add ice to this?
¿Puedes añadirle hielo?
PWEH-dehs ah-nyah-DEER-leh ee-EH-loh

I would like to order a dark beer.
Quisiera ordenar una cerveza oscura.
Kee-see-EH-rah ohr-deh-NAHR OO-nah sehr-VEH-sah ohs-KOO-rah.

Do you have any beer from the tap?
¿Tienen cerveza de barril?
Tee-EH-nehn sehr-VEH-sah deh bah-RREEL

How expensive is your champagne?
¿Cuánto cuesta la champaña?
KWAHN-toh KWEHS-tah lah chahm-PAH-nyah

Enjoy your meal.
Buen provecho.
Bwehn proh-VEH-choh.

I want this.
Quiero esto.
Kee-EH-roh EHS-toh

Please cook my meat well done.
Mi carne bien cocida, por favor.
Mee KAHR-neh bee-EHN koh-SEE-dah, pohr fah-VOHR

Please cook my meat medium rare.
Mi carne a término medio, por favor.
Mee KAHR-neh ah TEHR-mee-noh MEH-dee-oh, pohr fah-VOHR

Please prepare my meat rare.
Mi carne casi cruda, por favor.
Mee KAHR-neh kah-see KROO-dah, pohr fah-VOHR

What type of fish do you serve?
¿Qué tipo de pescado tienen?
Keh TEE-poh deh pehs-KAH-doh tee-EH-nehn

Can I make a substitution with my meal?
¿Puedo hacer una sustitución en mi comida?
PWEH-doh ah-SEHR OO-nah soos-tee-too-see-OHN ehn mee koh-MEE-dah

Do you have a booster seat for my child?
¿Tienen sillas para bebés?
Tee-EH-nehn SEE-yahs PAH-rah beh-BEHS

Call us when you get a table.
Llámanos cuando consigas una mesa.
YAH-mah-nohs KWAHN-do kohn-SEE-gahs OO-nah MEH-sah

Is this a no smoking section?
¿Esta es un área para no fumadores?
EHS-tah ehs oon AH-reh-ah PAH-rah noh foo-mah-DOH-rehs

We would like to be seated in the smoking section.
Nos gustaría sentarnos en la sección de fumadores.
Nohs goos-tah-REE-ah sehn-tahr-nohs ehn lah sehk-see-OHN deh foo-mah-DOH-rehs

This meat tastes funny.
Esta carne está rara.
EHS-tah KAHR-neh ehs-TAH RRAH-rah

More people will be joining us later.
Luego vendrán más personas.
LWEH-goh vehn-DRAHN mahs pehr-SOH-nahs

TRANSPORTATION

Where's the train station?
¿Dónde está la estación de trenes?
DOHN-deh ehs-TAH lah ehs-tah-see-OHN deh TREH-nehs

How much does it cost to get to this address?
¿Cuánto cuesta llegar a esta dirección?
KWAHN-toh KWEHS-tah yeh-GAHR ah EHS-tah dee-rehk-see-OHN

Do you have first class tickets available?
¿Tienes boletos de primera clase disponibles?
Tee-EH-nehs boh-LEH-tohs deh pree-MEH-rah KLAH-seh dees-poh-NEE-blehs

What platform do I need to be on to catch this train?
¿En qué plataforma debo estar para tomar el tren?
Ehn keh plah-tah-FOHR-mah DEH-boh ehs-TAHR PAH-rah toh-MAHR ehl trehn

Are the roads paved in this area?
¿Las carreteras están pavimentadas en esta área?
Lahs kah-rreh-TEH-rahs ehs-TAHN pah-vee-mehn-TAH-dahs ehn EHS-tah AH-reh-ah

Where are the dirt roads and how do I avoid them?
¿Dónde están las carreteras de tierra y cómo puedo evitarlas?
DOHN-deh ehs-TAHN lahs kah-rreh-TEH-rahs deh tee-EH-rrah ee KOH-moh PWEH-doh eh-vee-TAHR-lahs

Are there any potholes I need to avoid?
¿Hay baches que deba evitar?
AH-ee BAH-chehs keh DEH-bah eh-vee-TAHR

How fast are you going?
¿Qué tan rápido vas?
Keh tahn RRAH-pee-doh vahs

Do I need to put my emergency blinkers on?
¿Necesito encender las luces intermitentes de emergencia?
Neh-seh-SEE-toh ehn-sehn-DEHR lahs LOO-sehs een-tehr-mee-TEHN-tehs deh eh-mehr-HEHN-see-ah

Make sure to use the right turn signals.
Asegúrate de usar la luz direccional correcta.
Ah-see-GOO-rah-teh deh oo-SAHR lah loos dee-rehk-see-oh-NAHL koh-RREHK-tah

We need a good mechanic.
Necesitamos un buen mecánico.
Neh-seh-see-TAH-mohs oon bwehn meh-KAH-nee-koh

Can we get a push?
¿Puedes darnos un empujoncito?
PWEH-dehs DAHR-nohs oon ehm-poo-hohn-SEE-toh

I have to call the towing company to move my car.
Tengo que llamar a la compañía de grúas para mover mi auto.
TEHN-goh keh yah-MAHR ah lah kohm-pah-NYEE-ah deh GROO-ahs PAH-rah moh-VEHR mee AH-oo-toh

Make sure to check the battery and spark plugs for any problems.
Asegúrate de revisar la batería y las bujías por si acaso.
Ah-seh-GOO-rah-teh deh rreh-vee-SAHR lah bah-teh-REE-ah ee lahs boo-HEE-ahs pohr see ah-KAH-soh

Check the oil level.
Revisa el nivel del aceite.
Rreh-VEE-sah ehl nee-VEHL dehl ah-SEH-ee-teh

I need to notify my insurance company.
Necesito notificar a mi compañía de seguros.
Neh-seh-SEE-toh noh-tee-fee-KAHR ah mee kohm-pah-NYEE-ah deh seh-GOO-rohs

When do I pay the taxi driver?
¿Cuándo le pago al taxista?
KWAHN-doh leh PAH-goh ahl tak-SEES-tah

Please take me to the nearest train station.
Por favor, llévame a la estación de trenes más cercana.
Pohr fah-VOHR, YEH-vah-meh ah lah ehs-tah-see-OHN deh TREH-nehs
mahs sehr-KAH-nah

How long does it take to get to this address?
¿Cuánto tiempo toma llegar a esta dirección?
KWAHN-toh tee-EHM-poh TOH-mah yeh-GAHR ah EHS-tah dee-rehk-
see-OHN

Can you stop here, please?
¿Puedes detenerte aquí?
PWEH-dehs deh-teh-NEHR-teh ah-KEE

You can drop me off anywhere around here.
Puedes dejarme por aquí.
PWEH-dehs deh-HAHR-meh pohr ah-KEE

Is there a charge for extra passengers?
¿Debo pagar extra por otros pasajeros?
DEH-boh pah-GAHR EHKS-trah pohr OH-trohs pah-sah-HEH-rohs

What is the condition of the road? Is it safe to travel there?
¿En qué condición está la carretera? ¿Es seguro viajar allí?
Ehn keh kohn-dee-see-OHN ehs-TAH lah kah-rreh-TEH-rah. Ehs seh-
GOO-roh vee-ah-HAR ah-YEE

Take me to the emergency room.
Llévame a la sala de emergencias.
YEH-vah-meh ah lah SAH-lah deh eh-mehr-HEHN-see-ahs

Take me to the embassy.
Llévame a la embajada.

YEH-vah-meh ah lah ehm-bah-HAH-dah

I want to travel around the country.
Quiero viajar por el país.
Kee-EH-roh vee-ah-HAHR pohr ehl pah-EES

Is this the right side of the road?
¿Este es el lado correcto de la carretera?
EHS-teh ehs ehl LAH-doh koh-RREHK-toh deh lah kah-rreh-TEH-rah

My car broke down, please help!
¡Ayuda, mi auto se dañó!
Ah-YOO-dah, mee AH-oo-toh seh dah-NYOH

Can you help me change my tire?
¿Puedes ayudarme a cambiar el neumático?
PWEH-dehs ah-yoo-DAHR-meh ah kahm-bee-AHR ehl neh-oo-MAH-tee-koh

Where can I get a rental car?
¿Dónde puedo conseguir un auto de alquiler?
DOHN-deh PWEH-doh kohn-seh-GEER oon AH-oo-toh deh ahl-kee-LEHR

Please take us to the hospital.
Por favor, llévanos al hospital.
Pohr fah-VOHR, YEH-vah-nohs ahl ohs-pee-TAHL

Is that the car rental office?
¿Esa es la oficina para rentar autos?
EH-sah ehs lah oh-fee-SEE-nah PAH-rah RREHN-tahr AH-oo-tohs

May I have a price list for your fleet?
¿Puedo tener una lista de precios de su flota de autos?
PWEH-doh teh-NEHR OO-nah LEES-tah deh PREH-see-ohs deh soo FLOH-tah deh AH-oo-tohs

Can I get insurance on this rental car?
¿Puedo conseguir un seguro para este auto de alquiler?
PWEH-doh kohn-seh-GEER oon seh-GOO-roh PAH-rah EHS-teh AH-oo-toh deh ahl-kee-LEHR

How much is the car per day?
¿Cuánto cuesta el auto por día?
KWAHN-toh KWEHS-tah ehl AH-oo-tohs RREHN-tah pohr DEE-ah

How many kilometers can I travel with this car?
¿Cuántos kilómetros puedo recorrer con este auto?

KWAHN-tohs kee-LOH-meh-trohs PWEH-doh rreh-koh-RREHR kohn EHS-teh AH-oo-toh

I would like maps of the region if you have them.
Quisiera unos mapas de la región, si los tienes.
Kee-see-EH-rah OO-nohs MAH-pahs deh lah rreh-hee-OHN, see lohs tee-EH-nehs

When I am done with the car where do I return it?
¿Adónde debo regresar el auto cuando ya termine de usarlo?
Ah-DOHN-deh DEH-boh rreh-greh-SAHR ehl AH-oo-toh cuh-ahn-doh yah
tehr-meeh-neh deh oo-sahr-loh

Is this a standard or automatic transmission?
¿Es de transmisión manual o automática?
Ehs deh trahns-mee-see-OHN mah-noo-AHL oh ah-oo-toh-MAH-tee-kah

Is this car gas efficient? How many kilometers per liter?
¿Este auto consume mucha gasolina? ¿Cuántos kilómetros recorre por
litro?
EHS-teh AH-oo-toh kohn-SOO-meh MOO-chah gah-soh-LEE-nah.
KWAHN-tohs kee-LOH-meh-trohs rreh-KOH-rreh pohr LEE-troh

Where is the spare tire stored?
¿Dónde está guardado el neumático de repuesto?
DOHN-deh ehs-TAH goo-ahr-DAH-doh ehl neh-oo-MAH-tee-koh deh
rreh-PWEHS-toh

Are there places around the city that are difficult to drive?
¿Hay lugares en los alrededores de la ciudad donde sea difícil conducir?
AH-ee loo-GAH-rehs ehn lohs ahl-rreh-deh-DOH-rehs deh lah see-oo-
DAHD DOHN-deh SEH-ah dee-FEE-seel kohn-doo-SEER

At what time of the day is the traffic the worst?
¿Cuál es la peor hora del tráfico?
Kwahl ehs lah peh-OHR OH-rah dehl TRAH-fee-koh

We can't park right here.
No podemos estacionarnos aquí.
Noh poh-DEH-mohs ehs-tah-see-oh-NAHR-nohs ah-KEE

What is the speed limit?
¿Cuál es el límite de velocidad?
Kwahl ehs ehl LEE-mee-teh deh veh-loh-see-DAHD

Keep the change.
Quédate con el cambio.
KEH-dah-teh kohn ehl KAHM-bee-oh

Now let's get off here.
Vámonos de aquí.
VAH-moh-nohs deh ah-KEE

Is the bus stop nearby?
¿La estación de buses está cerca?
Lah ehs-tah-see-OHN deh BOO-sehs ehs-TAH SEHR-kah

When does the bus run?
¿A qué hora pasa el bus?
Ah keh OH-rah PAH-sah ehl boos

Where do I go to catch a taxi?
¿Dónde puedo tomar un taxi?
DOHN-deh PWEH-doh toh-MAHR oon TAHK-see

Does the train go to the north station?
¿El tren va a la estación norte?
Ehl trehn vah ah lah ehs-tah-see-OHN NOHR-teh

Where do I go to purchase tickets?
¿Dónde compro los boletos?
DOHN-deh KOHM-proh lohs boh-LEH-tohs

How much is a ticket to the north?
¿Cuánto cuesta un boleto hacia el norte?
KWAHN-toh KWEHS-tah oon boh-LEH-toh AH-see-ah ehl NOHR-teh

What is the next stop along this route?
¿Cuál es la siguiente parada en la ruta?
Kwahl ehs lah see-gee-EHN-teh pah-RAH-dah ehn lah RROO-tah

Can I have a ticket to the north?
¿Me das un boleto hacia el norte?
Meh dahs oon boh-LEH-toh AH-see-ah ehl NOHR-teh

Where is my designated platform?
¿Dónde está mi plataforma designada?
DOHN-deh ehs-TAH mee plah-tah-FOHR-mah deh-seeg-NAH-dah

Where do I place my luggage?
¿Dónde coloco mi equipaje?
DOHN-deh koh-LOH-koh mee eh-kee-PAH-heh

Are there any planned closures today?
¿Hay cierres programados para hoy?
AH-ee see-EH-rrehs proh-grah-MAH-dohs PAH-rah OH-ee

Where are the machines that dispense tickets?
¿Dónde está la máquina que entrega los boletos?
DOHN-deh ehs-TAH lah MAH-kee-nah keh ehn-TREH-gah lohs boh-LEH-tohs

Does this car come with insurance?
¿Este auto viene con seguro?
EHS-teh AH-oo-toh vee-EH-neh kohn seh-GOO-roh

May I have a timetable, please?
¿Me muestras un horario, por favor?
Meh moo-EHS-trahs oon oh-RAH-ree-oh, pohr fah-VOHR

How often do trains come to this area?
¿Cada cuánto tiempo pasan los trenes por aquí?
KAH-dah KWAHN-toh tee-EHM-poh PAH-sahn lohs TREH-nehs pohr ah-KEE

Is the train running late?
¿El tren está retrasado?
Ehl trehn ehs-TAH ah-trah-SAH-doh

Has the train been cancelled?
¿Cancelaron el tren?
Kahn-seh-LAH-rohn ehl trehn

Is this seat available?
¿Este asiento está libre?
EHS-teh ah-see-EHN-toh ehs-TAH LEE-breh

Do you mind if I sit here?
¿Te importa si me siento aquí?
Teh eem-POHR-tah see meh see-EHN-toh ah-KEE

I've lost my ticket.
Perdí mi boleto.
Pehr-DEE mee boh-LEH-toh

Excuse me, this is my stop.
Disculpe, esta es mi parada.
Dees-KOOL-peh, EHS-tah ehs mee pah-RAH-dah

Can you please open the window?
¿Puedes abrir la ventana, por favor?
PWEH-dehs ah-BREER lah vehn-TAH-nah, pohr fah-VOHR

Is smoking allowed in the car?
¿Está permitido fumar dentro del carro?
Ehs-TAH pehr-mee-TEE-doh foo-MAHR DEHN-troh dehl KAH-rroh

Keep the change.
Quédate con el cambio.
KEH-dah-teh kohn ehl KAHM-bee-oh

Wait, my luggage is still onboard!
¡Espera, mis maletas siguen a bordo!
Ehs-PEH-rah, mees mah-LEH-tahs SEE-gehn ah BOHR-doh

Where can I get a map?
¿Dónde puedo conseguir un mapa?
DOHN-deh PWEH-doh kohn-seh-GEER oon MAH-pah

What zone is this?
¿Qué zona es esta?
Keh SOH-nah ehs EHS-tah

Please be careful of the gap!
¡Ten cuidado con los huecos, por favor!
Tehn koo-ee-DAH-doh kohn lohs oo-EH-kohs, pohr fah-VOHR

I am about to run out of gas.
Estoy a punto de quedarme sin gasolina.
Ehs-TOH-ee ah POON-toh deh keh-DAHR-meh seen gah-soh-LEE-nah

My tank is halfway full.
Mi tanque está medio lleno.
Mee TAHN-keh ehs-TAH MEH-dee-oh YEH-noh

What type of gas does this car take?
¿Qué tipo de gasolina usa este auto?
Keh TEE-poh deh gah-soh-LEE-nah OO-sah EHS-teh AH-oo-toh

There is gas leaking out of my car.
Hay una fuga de gasolina en mi auto.
AH-ee OO-nah FOO-gah deh gah-soh-LEE-nah ehn mee AH-oo-toh.

Fill up the tank.
Llena el tanque.
YEH-nah ehl TAHN-keh

There is no more gas in my car.
Mi auto no tiene gasolina.
Mee AH-oo-toh noh tee-EH-neh gah-soh-LEE-nah

Where can I find the nearest gas station?
¿Dónde está la gasolinera más cercana?
DOHN-deh ehs-TAH lah gah-soh-lee-NEH-rah mahs sehr-KAH-nah

The engine light for my car is on.
La luz de revisión del motor de mi auto está encendida.
Lah loos deh rreh-vee-see-OHN dehl moh-TOHR deh mee AH-oo-toh
ehs-TAH ehn-sehn-DEE-dah

Do you mind if I drive?
¿Te importa si conduzco?
Teh eem-POHR-tah see kohn-DOOS-koh

Please get in the back seat.
Por favor, siéntate atrás.
Pohr fah-VOHR, see-EHN-tah-teh ah-TRAHS

Let me get my bags out before you leave.
Déjame sacar mi equipaje antes de que te vayas.
DEH-hah-meh sah-KAHR mee eh-kee-PAH-heh AHN-tehs deh keh teh
VAH-yahs

The weather is bad, please drive slowly.
El clima no es bueno, por favor, conduce despacio.
Ehl KLEE-mah noh ehs BWEH-noh, pohr fah-VOHR, kohn-DOO-seh dehs-
PAH-see-oh

Our vehicle isn't equipped to travel there.
Nuestro auto no está equipado para viajar allí.
NWEHS-troh AH-oo-toh noh ehs-TAH eh-kee-PAH-doh PAH-rah vee-ah-
HAHR ah-YEE

One ticket to the north, please.
Un boleto hacia el norte, por favor.
Oon boh-LEH-toh AH-see-ah ehl NOHR-teh, pohr fah-VOHR

If you get lost, call me.
Si te pierdes, llámame.
See teh pee-EHR-dehs, YAH-mah-meh

That bus is overcrowded. I will wait for the next one.
Ese bus está muy lleno. Esperaré el próximo.
EH-seh boos ehs-TAH MOO-ee YEH-noh. Ehs-peh-rah-REH ehl PROHK-see-moh

Please, take my seat.
Por favor, toma mi asiento.
Pohr fah-VOHR, TOH-mah mee ah-see-EHN-toh

Ma'am, I think your stop is coming up.
Señora, creo que estamos llegando a su parada.
Seh-NYOH-rah, KREH-oh keh ehs-TAH-mohs yeh-GAHN-doh ah soo pah-RAH-dah

Wake me up when we get to our destination.
Despiértame cuando lleguemos a nuestro destino.
Dehs-pee-EHR-tah-meh KWAHN-doh yeh-GEH-mohs ah NWEHS-troh dehs-TEE-noh

I would like to purchase a travel pass for the entire day.
Quisiera comprar un boleto de viaje para todo el día.
Kee-see-EH-rah kohm-PRAHR oon boh-LEH-toh deh vee-AH-heh PAH-rah TOH-doh ehl DEE-ah

Would you like to swap seats with me?
¿Te gustaría intercambiar asientos conmigo?
Teh goos-tah-REE-ah een-tehr-kahm-bee-AHR ah-see-EHN-tohs kohn-MEE-goh

I want to sit with my family.
Quiero sentarme con mi familia.
Kee-EH-roh sehn-TAHR-meh kohn mee fah-MEE-lee-ah

I would like a window seat for this trip.
Quisiera un asiento con ventanilla para este viaje.
Kee-see-EH-rah oon ah-see-EHN-toh kohn vehn-tah-NEE-yah PAH-rah EHS-teh vee-AH-heh

RELIGIOUS QUESTIONS

Where can I go to pray?
¿Dónde puedo ir a orar?
DOHN-deh PWEH-doh eer ah oh-RAHR

What services does your church offer?
¿Qué servicios ofrece su iglesia?
Keh sehr-VEE-see-ohs oh-FREH-seh soo ee-GLEH-see-ah

Are you non-denominational?
¿Ustedes son no confesionales?
Oos-TEH-dehs sohn noh kohn-feh-see-oh-NAH-lehs

Is there a shuttle to your church?
¿Hay un transporte hacia su iglesia?
AH-ee oon trahns-POHR-teh AH-see-ah soo ee-GLEH-see-ah

How long does church last?
¿Cuánto dura la misa?
KWAHN-toh DOO-rah lah MEE-sah

Where is your bathroom?
¿Dónde está su baño?
DOHN-deh ehs-TAH soo BAH-nyoh

What should I wear to your services?
¿Cómo debo vestir para sus servicios?
KOH-moh DEH-boh vehs-TEER PAH-rah soos sehr-VEE-see-ohs

Where is the nearest Catholic Church?
¿Dónde está la iglesia católica más cercana?
DOHN-deh ehs-TAH lah ee-GLEH-see-ah kah-TOH-lee-kah mahs sehr-KAH-nah

Where is the nearest Mosque?
¿Dónde está la mezquita más cercana?
DOHN-deh ehs-TAH lah mehs-KEE-tah mahs sehr-KAH-nah

Does your church perform weddings?
¿Su iglesia realiza bodas?
Soo ee-GLEH-see-ah rreh-ah-LEE-sah BOH-dahs

Who is getting married?
¿Quién se casa?
Kee-EHN seh KAH-sah

Will our marriage license be legal if we leave the country?
¿Nuestra licencia de matrimonio será legal si dejamos el país?
NWEHS-trah lee-SEHN-see-ah deh mah-tree-MOH-nee-oh seh-RAH leh-GAHL see deh-HAH-mohs ehl pah-EES

Where do we get our marriage license?
¿Dónde podemos obtener nuestra licencia de matrimonio?
DOHN-deh poh-DEH-mohs ohb-teh-NEHR NWEHS-trah lee-SEHN-see-ah deh mah-tree-MOH-nee-oh

What is the charge for marrying us?
¿Cuánto cuesta casarnos?
KWAHN-toh KWEHS-tah kah-SAHR-nohs

Do you handle same sex marriage?
¿Realizan matrimonios del mismo sexo?
Rreh-ah-LEE-sahn mah-tree-MOH-nee-ohs dehl MEES-moh SEHK-soh

Please gather here to pray.
Por favor, reúnanse aquí para orar.
Pohr fah-VOHR, rreh-OO-nahn-seh ah-KEE PAH-rah oh-RAHR

I would like to lead a sermon.
Quisiera dirigir un sermón.
Kee-see-EH-rah dee-ree-HEER oon sehr-MOHN

I would like to help with prayer.
Quisiera ayudar con la oración.
Kee-see-EH-rah ah-yoo-DAHR kohn lah oh-rah-see-OHN

How should I dress before arriving?
¿Cómo debería vestirme antes de llegar?
KOH-moh deh-beh-REE-ah vehs-TEER-meh AHN-tehs deh yeh-GAHR

What are your rules?
¿Cuáles son sus reglas?
KWAH-lehs sohn soos RREH-glahs

Are cell phones allowed in your building?
¿Están permitidos los celulares?
Ehs-TAHN pehr-mee-TEE-dohs lohs seh-loo-LAH-rehs

I plan on bringing my family this Sunday.
Planeo traer a mi familia este domingo.
Plah-NEH-oh trah-EHR ah mee fah-MEE-lee-ah EHS-teh doh-MEEN-goh

Do you accept donations?
¿Ustedes aceptan donaciones?
Oos-TEH-dehs ah-SEHP-tahn doh-nah-see-OH-nehs

I would like to offer my time to your cause.
Quisiera ofrecer mi tiempo para su causa.
Kee-see-EH-rah oh-freh-SEHR mee tee-EHM-poh PAH-rah soo KAH-oo-sah

What book should I be reading from?
¿Qué libro debería leer?
Keh LEE-broh deh-beh-REE-ah leh-EHR

Do you have a gift store?
¿Tienen tienda de regalos?
Tee-EH-nehn tee-EHN-dah deh rreh-GAH-lohs

EMERGENCY

I need help over here!
¡Necesito ayuda aquí!
Neh-seh-SEE-toh ah-YOO-dah ah-KEE

I'm lost, please help me.
Estoy perdido, por favor, ayúdame.
Ehs-TOH-ee pehr-DEE-doh, pohr fah-VOHR, ah-YOO-dah-meh

Someone call the police!
¡Llamen a la policía!
YAH-mehn ah lah poh-lee-SEE-ah

Is there a lawyer who speaks English?
¿Hay algún abogado aquí que hable inglés?
AH-ee ahl-GOON ah-boh-GAH-doh ah-KEE keh AH-bleh een-GLEHS

Please help, my car doesn't work.
Por favor, ayúdame, mi auto no funciona.
Pohr fah-VOHR, ah-YOO-dah-meh, mee AH-oo-toh noh foon-see-OH-nah

There was a collision!
¡Hubo un accidente!
OO-boh oon ahk-see-DEHN-teh

Call an ambulance!
¡Llamen a una ambulancia!
YAH-mehn ah OO-nah ahm-boo-LAHN-see-ah

Am I under arrest?
¿Estoy bajo arresto?
Ehs-TOH-ee BAH-oh ah-RREHS-toh

I need an interpreter; this is an emergency!
Necesito un intérprete, ¡esto es una emergencia!
Neh-seh-SEE-toh oon een-TEHR-preh-teh, ehs-toh ehs OO-nah eh-mehr-HEHN-see-ah

My back hurts.
Me duele la espalda.
Meh doo-EH-leh lah ehs-PAHL-dah

Is there an American consulate here?
¿Hay un consulado americano aquí?
AH-ee oon kohn-soo-LAH-doh ah-meh-ree-KAH-noh ah-KEE

I'm sick and don't feel too well.
Estoy enfermo y no me siento muy bien.
Ehs-TOH-ee ehn-FEHR-moh ee noh meh see-EHN-toh MOO-ee bee-EHN

Is there a pharmacy where I can get medicine?
¿Hay una farmacia por aquí donde pueda conseguir medicina?
AH-ee OO-nah fahr-MAH-see-ah pohr ah-KEE DOHN-deh PWEH-dah
kohn-seh-GEER meh-dee-SEE-nah

I need a doctor immediately.
Necesito un doctor inmediatamente.
Neh-seh-SEE-toh oon dohk-TOHR een-meh-dee-ahn-tah-MEHN-teh

I have a tooth missing.
Perdí un diente.
Pehr-DEE oon dee-EHN-teh

Please! Someone bring my child to me!
¡Por favor!, ¡Tráiganme a mi niño!
Pohr fah-VOHR, TRAH-ee-gahn-meh ah mee NEE-nyoh

Where does it hurt?
¿Dónde te duele?
DOHN-deh teh doo-EH-leh

Hold on to me!
¡Agárrate a mí!
Ah-GAH-rrah-teh ah mee

There's an emergency!
¡Hay una emergencia!
AH-ee OO-nah eh-mehr-HEHN-see-ah

I need a telephone to call for help.
Necesito un teléfono para pedir ayuda.
Neh-seh-SEE-toh oon teh-LEH-foh-noh PAH-rah peh-DEER ah-YOO-dah

My nose is bleeding.
Me sangra la nariz.
Meh SAHN-grah lah nah-REES

I twisted my ankle.
Me doblé el tobillo.
Meh doh-BLEH ehl toh-BEE-yoh

I don't feel so good.
No me siento muy bien.
Noh meh see-EHN-toh MOO-ee bee-EHN

Don't move, please.
Por favor, no te muevas.
Pohr fah-VOHR, noh teh moo-EH-vahs

Hello operator, can I place a collect call?
Hola operador, ¿puedo hacer una llamada por cobrar?
OH-lah oh-peh-rah-DOHR, PWEH-doh ah-SEHR OO-nah yah-MAH-dah
pohr koh-BRAHR

I'll get a doctor for you.
Te conseguiré un doctor.
Teh kohn-seh-gee-REH oon dohk-TOHR

Please hold my passport for a while.
Por favor, sostén mi pasaporte un rato.
Pohr fah-VOHR, sohs-TEHN mee pah-sah-POHR-teh oon RRAH-toh

I lost my wallet.
Perdí mi billetera.
Pehr-DEE mee bee-yeh-TEH-rah

I have a condition! Please check my wallet.
¡Tengo una condición! Por favor, revisa mi billetera.
TEHN-goh OO-nah kohn-dee-see-OHN. Pohr fah-VOHR, rreh-VEE-sah
mee bee-yeh-TEH-rah

My wife is in labor please help!
¡Mi esposa está dando a luz, ayuda!
Mee ehs-POH-sah ehs-TAH DAHN-doh ah loos, ah-YOO-dah

I would like to talk to my lawyer.
Me gustaría hablar con mi abogado.
Meh goos-tah-REE-ah ah-BLAHR kohn mee ah-boh-GAH-doh

It's an earthquake!

¡Es un terremoto!

Ehs oon teh-rreh-MOH-toh

Get under the desk and protect your head.

¡Métete bajo el escritorio y protege tu cabeza!

MEH-teh-teh BAH-hoh ehl ehs-kree-TOH-ree-oh ee proh-TEH-heh too
kah-BEH-sah

How can I help you?

¿Cómo puedo ayudarte?

KOH-moh PWEH-doh ah-yoo-DAHR-teh

Everyone, he needs help!

¡Oigan todos, él necesita ayuda!

OH-ee-gahn TOH-dohs ehl neh-seh-SEE-tah ah-YOO-dah

Yes, help me get an ambulance.

Sí, ayúdame a encontrar una ambulancia.

See, ah-YOO-dah-meh ah ehn-kohn-TRAHR OO-nah ahm-boo-LAHN-see-
ah

Thank you, but I am fine. Please don't help me.

Gracias, pero estoy bien. Por favor, no me ayudes.

GRAH-see-ahs, PEH-roh ehs-TOH-ee bee-EHN. Pohr fah-VOHR, noh meh
ah-YOO-dehs

I need help carrying this injured person.

Necesito ayuda con esta persona herida.

Neh-seh-SEE-toh ah-YOO-dah kohn EHS-tah pehr-SOH-nah eh-REE-dah

TECHNOLOGY

What is the country's official website?
¿Cuál es la página web oficial del país?
Kwahl ehs lah PAH-hee-nah web oh-fee-see-AHL dehl pah-EES

Do you know the name of a good Wi-Fi café?
¿Sabes el nombre de una buena cafetería con Wi-Fi?
SAH-behs ehl NOHM-breh deh OO-nah BWEH-nah kah-feh-teh-REE-ah kohn Wi-Fi

Do you have any experience with computers?
¿Tienes alguna experiencia con computadores?
Tee-EH-nehs ahl-GOO-nah ehks-peh-ree-EHN-see-ah kohn kohm-poo-tah-DOH-rehs

How well do you know Apple products?
¿Qué tanto conoces los productos de Apple?
Keh TAHN-toh koh-NOH-sehs lohs proh-DOOK-tohs deh Apple

What kind of work did you do with computers?
¿Qué tipo de trabajo hiciste con los computadores?
Keh TEE-poh deh trah-BAH-hoh ee-SEES-teh kohn lohs kohm-poo-tah-DOH-rehs

Are you a programmer?
¿Eres programador?
EH-rehs proh-grah-mah-DOHR

Are you a developer?
¿Eres desarrollador?
EH-rehs deh-sah-rroh-yah-DOHR

I want to use that computer instead of that one.
Prefiero usar este computador en vez de aquel.
Preh-fee-EH-roh oo-SAHR EHS-teh kohm-poo-tah-DOHR ehn vehs deh ah-KEHL

Do you know where I can buy discount computer parts?
¿Sabes dónde puedo comprar partes de computador con descuento?
SAH-behs DOHN-deh PWEH-doh kohm-PRAHR PAHR-tehs deh kohm-poo-tah-DOHR kohn dehs-koo-EHN-toh

I have ten years' experience with Windows.
Tengo diez años de experiencia con Windows.
TEHN-goh dee-EHS AH-nyohs deh ehks-peh-ree-EHN-see-ah kohn Windows.

What is the Wi-Fi password?
¿Cuál es la contraseña del Wi-Fi?
Kwahl ehs lah kohn-trah-SEH-nyah dehl Wi-Fi

I need to have my login information reset.
Necesito restablecer mi información para iniciar sesión.
Neh-seh-SEE-toh rrehs-tah-bleh-SEHR mee een-fohr-mah-see-OHN PAH-rah ee-nee-see-AHR seh-see-OHN

The hard drive is making a clicking noise.
El disco duro está haciendo un ruido como un chasquido.
Ehl DEES-koh DOO-roh ehs-TAH ah-see-EHN-doh oon rroo-EE-doh KOH-moh oon chahs-KEE-doh

How do I uninstall this program from my device?
¿Cómo desinstalo este programa de mi dispositivo?
KOH-moh dehs-eens-TAH-loh EHS-teh proh-GRAH-mah deh mee dees-poh-see-TEE-voh

Can you help me set up a new account with this website?
¿Puedes ayudarme a abrir una cuenta nueva para esta página web?
PWEH-dehs ah-yoo-DAHR-meh ah ah-BREER OO-nah KWEHN-tah NWEH-vah PAH-rah EHS-tah PAH-hee-nah web

Why is the internet so slow?
¿Por qué está tan lento el internet?
Pohr keh ehs-TAH tahn LEHN-toh ehl een-tehr-NEHT

Why is YouTube buffering every video I play?
¿Por qué YouTube tarda en cargar cada video que reproduzco?
Pohr keh YouTube TAHR-dah ehn kahr-GAHR KAH-dah vee-DEH-oh keh rreh-proh-DOOS-koh

My web camera isn't displaying a picture.
Mi cámara web no muestra ninguna imagen.
Mee KAH-mah-rah web noh moo-EHS-trah neen-GOO-nah ee-MAH-hehn

I have no bars on my phone.
No tengo señal en mi teléfono.
Noh TEHN-goh seh-NYAHL ehn mee teh-LEH-foh-noh

Where can I get my phone serviced?
¿Dónde puedo reparar mi teléfono?
DOHN-deh PWEH-doh rreh-pah-RAHR mee teh-LEH-foh-noh

My phone shows that it is charging but won't charge.
Mi teléfono muestra que está cargando, pero en realidad no carga.
Mee teh-LEH-foh-noh moo-EHS-trah keh ehs-TAH kahr-GAHN-doh, PEH-roh ehn rreh-ah-lee-DAHD noh KAHR-gah

I think someone else is controlling my computer.
Creo que alguien más está controlando mi computador.
KREH-oh keh AHL-gee-ehn mahs ehs-TAH kohn-troh-LAHN-doh mee kohm-poo-tah-DOHR

My computer just gave a blue screen and shut down.
Mi computador solo mostró una pantalla azul y se apagó.
Mee kohm-poo-tah-DOHR SOH-loh mohs-TROH OO-nah pahn-TAH-yah ah-SOOL ee seh ah-pah-GOH

Do you have the battery for this laptop?
¿Tienes la batería para este portátil?
Tee-EH-nehs lah bah-teh-REE-ah PAH-rah EHS-teh pohr-TAH-teel

Where can I get a compatible adapter?
¿Dónde puedo conseguir un adaptador compatible?
DOHN-deh PWEH-doh kohn-seh-GEER oon ah-dahp-tah-DOR kohm-pah-TEE-bleh

I can't get online with the information you gave me.
No puedo conectarme a internet con la información que me diste.
Noh PWEH-doh koh-nehk-TAHR-meh ah een-tehr-NEHT kohn lah een-fohr-mah-see-OHN keh meh DEES-teh

This keyboard is not working correctly.
Este teclado no funciona correctamente.
EHS-teh teh-KLAH-doh noh foon-see-OH-nah koh-rrehk-tah-MEHN-teh

What is the login information for this computer?
¿Cuál es la información de inicio de sesión en este computador?
Kwahl ehs lah een-fohr-mah-see-OHN deh ee-NEE-see-oh deh seh-see-OHN ehn EHS-teh kohm-poo-tah-DOHR

I need you to update my computer.
Necesito que actualices mi computador.
Neh-seh-SEE-toh keh ahk-too-ah-LEE-sehs mee kohm-poo-tah-DOHR

Can you build my website?
¿Puedes construirme una página web?
PWEH-dehs kohns-troo-EER-meh OO-nah PAH-hee-nah web

I would prefer Wordpress.
Preferiría Wordpress.
Preh-feh-ree-REE-ah Wordpress.

What are your rates per hour?
¿Cuánto cobras por hora?
KWAHN-toh KOH-brahs pohr OH-rah

Do you have experience handling email servers?
¿Tienes experiencia manejando servidores de correo electrónico?
Tee-EH-nehs ehks-peh-ree-EHN-see-ah mah-neh-HAHN-doh sehr-vee-DOH-rehs deh koh-RREH-oh eh-lehk-TROH-nee-koh

I am locked out of my account, can you help?
Estoy bloqueado de mi cuenta, ¿puedes ayudarme?
Ehs-TOH-ee bloh-keh-AH-doh deh mee koo-EHN-tah, PWEH-dehs ah-yoo-DAHR-meh

None of the emails I am sending are going through.
Ninguno de los correos electrónicos que envío está llegando.
Neen-GOO-noh deh lohs koh-RREH-ohs eh-lehk-TROH-nee-kohs keh ehn-VEE-oh ehs-TAH yeh-GAHN-doh

The time and date on my computer are wrong.
La hora y fecha en mi computador son incorrectas.
Lah OH-rah ee FEH-chah ehn mee kohm-poo-tah-DOHR sohn een-koh-RREHK-tahs

Is this game free to play?
¿Este juego es gratuito?
EHS-teh hoo-EH-goh ehs grah-too-EE-toh

Where do I go to download the program?
¿Adónde voy para descargar el programa?
Ah-DOHN-deh VOH-ee PAH-rah dehs-kahr-GAHR ehl proh-GRAH-mah

I am having trouble chatting with my family.
Estoy teniendo problemas para chatear con mi familia.
Ehs-TOH-ee teh-nee-EHN-doh proh-BLEH-mahs PAH-rah chah-teh-AHR
kohn mee fah-MEE-lee-ah

Is this the fastest computer here?
¿Este es el computador más rápido que tienen?
EHS-teh ehs ehl kohm-poo-tah-DOHR mahs RRAH-pee-doh keh tee-EH-
nehn

How much space is on the computer?
¿Cuánto espacio tiene el computador?
KWAHN-toh ehs-PAH-see-oh tee-EH-neh ehl kohm-poo-tah-DOHR

Will my profile be deleted once I log out? Or does it save?
¿Se eliminará mi perfil cuando cierre sesión? ¿O quedará guardado?
Seh eh-lee-mee-nah-RAH mee pehr-FEEL KWAHN-doh see-EH-rreh seh-
see-OHN, oh keh-dah-RAH goo-ahr-DAH-doh

How much do you charge for computer use?
¿Cuánto cobras por usar el computador?
KWAHN-toh KOH-brahs pohr oo-SAHR ehl kohm-poo-tah-DOHR

Are group discounts offered?
¿Ofrecen descuentos a grupos?
Oh-FREH-sehn dehs-koo-EHN-tohs ah GROO-pohs

Can I use my own headphones with your computer?
¿Puedo usar mis propios audífonos en su computador?
PWEH-doh oo-SAHR mees PROH-pee-ohs ah-oo-DEE-foh-nohs ehn soo
kohm-poo-tah-DOHR

Do you have a data cap?
¿Tienen límite de datos?
Tee-EH-nehn LEE-mee-teh deh DAH-tohs

I think this computer has a virus.
Creo que este computador tiene un virus.
KREH-oh keh EHS-teh kohm-poo-tah-DOHR tee-EH-neh oon VEE-roos

The battery for my laptop is running low.
La batería de mi portátil está baja.
Lah bah-teh-REE-ah deh mee pohr-TAH-teel ehs-TAH BAH-hah

Where can I plug this in? I need to recharge my device.
¿Dónde puedo enchufar esto? Necesito cargar mi dispositivo.
DOHN-deh PWEH-doh ehn-choo-FAHR EHS-toh. Neh-seh-SEE-toh kahr-GAHR mee dees-poh-see-TEE-voh

Do you have a mini usb cord?
¿Tienes un cable mini USB?
Tee-EH-nehs oon KAH-bleh MEE-nee oo EH-seh beh

Where can I go to watch the game?
¿Adónde puedo ir para ver el juego?
Ah-DOHN-deh PWEH-doh eer PAH-rah vehr ehl hoo-EH-goh

Do you have an iPhone charger?
¿Tienes un cargador de iPhone?
Tee-EH-nehs oon kahr-gah-DOHR deh iPhone

I need a new battery for my watch.
Necesito una batería nueva para mi reloj.
Neh-seh-SEE-toh OO-nah bah-teh-REE-ah NWEH-vah PAH-rah mee rreh-LOH

I need to borrow an HDMI cord.
Necesito que me prestes un cable HDMI.
Neh-seh-SEE-toh keh meh PREHS-tehs oon KAH-bleh AH-cheh deh EH-meh ee

What happens when I exceed the data cap?
¿Qué pasa si excedo el límite de datos?
Keh PAH-sah see ehk-SEH-doh ehl LEE-mee-teh deh DAH-tohs

Can you help me pair my Bluetooth device?
¿Puedes ayudarme a conectar mi dispositivo Bluetooth?
PWEH-dehs ah-yoo-DAHR-meh ah koh-nehk-TAHR mee dees-poh-see-TEE-voh Bluetooth

I need a longer ethernet cord.
Necesito un cable de ethernet más largo.
Neh-seh-SEE-toh oon KAH-bleh deh ethernet mahs LAHR-goh

Why is this website restricted?
¿Por qué este sitio web está restringido?
Pohr keh EHS-teh SEE-tee-oh web ehs-TAH rrehs-treen-HEE-doh

How can I unblock this website?
¿Cómo puedo desbloquear este sitio web?
KOH-moh PWEH-doh dehs-bloh-keh-AHR EHS-teh SEE-tee-oh web

Is that television 4k or higher?
¿Ese televisor tiene una resolución de 4K o mejor?
EH-seh teh-leh-vee-SOHR tee-EH-neh OO-nah rreh-soh-loo-see-OHN deh
KWAH-troh kah oh meh-HOHR

Do you have the office suite on this computer?
¿Tienen el paquete ofimático en este computador?
Tee-EH-nehn ehl pah-KEH-teh oh-fee-MAH-tee-koh ehn EHS-teh kohm-
poo-tah-DOHR

This application won't install on my device.
Esta aplicación no se instala en mi dispositivo.
EHS-tah ah-plee-kah-see-OHN noh seh eens-TAH-lah ehn mee dees-poh-
see-TEE-voh

Can you change the channel on the television?
¿Puedes cambiar el canal de televisión?
PWEH-dehs kahm-bee-AHR ehl kah-NAHL deh teh-leh-vee-see-OHN

I think a fuse blew.
Creo que un fusible estalló.
KRE-oh keh oon foo-SEE-bleh ehs-tah-YOH

The screen is black and won't come on.
La pantalla está negra y no enciende.
Lah pahn-TAH-yah ehs-TAH NEH-grah ee noh ehn-see-EHN-deh

I keep getting popups on every website.
Me siguen saliendo ventanas emergentes en todos los sitios web.
Meh SEE-gehn sah-lee-EHN-doh vehn-TAH-nahs eh-mehr-HEHN-tehs
ehn TOH-dos lohs SEE-tee-ohs web

This computer is moving much slower than it should.
Este computador está funcionando mucho más lento de lo que debería.
EHS-teh kohm-poo-tah-DOHR ehs-TAH foon-see-oh-NAHN-doh MOO-choh mahs LEHN-toh deh loh keh deh-beh-REE-ah

I need to reactivate my copy of Windows.
Necesito reactivar mi copia de Windows.

Neh-seh-SEE-toh rreh-ahk-tee-VAHR mee KOH-pee-ah deh Windows

Why is this website blocked on my laptop?
¿Por qué este sitio web está bloqueado en mi portátil?

Pohr keh EHS-teh SEE-tee-oh web ehs-TAH bloh-keh-AH-doh ehn mee pohr-TAH-teel

Can you show me how to download videos to my computer?
¿Puedes mostrarme cómo descargar videos en mi computador?
PWEH-dehs mohs-TRAHR-meh KOH-moh dehs-kahr-GAHR vee-DEH-ohs ehn mee kohm-poo-tah-DOHR

Can I insert a flash drive into this computer?
¿Puedo insertar una memoria USB en este computador?
PWEH-doh een-sehr-TAHR OO-nah meh-MOH-ree-ah oo EH-seh beh ehn EHS-teh kohm-poo-tah-DOHR

I want to change computers.
Quiero cambiar de computador.
Kee-EH-roh kahm-bee-AHR deh kohm-poo-tah-DOHR

Is Chrome the only browser I can use with this computer?
¿Solo puedo usar Chrome como buscador en este computador?
SOH-loh PWEH-doh oo-SAHR Chrome KOH-moh boos-kah-DOHR ehn EHS-teh kohm-poo-tah-DOHR

Do you track my usage on any of these devices?
¿Controlan el uso que doy a alguno de estos dispositivos?

Kohn-TROH-lahn ehl OO-soh keh DOH-ee ah ahl-GOO-noh deh EHS-tohs des-poh-see-TEE-vohs

CONVERSATION TIPS

Pardon me.
Perdón.
Pehr-DOHN

Please speak more slowly.
Por favor, habla más lento.
Pohr fah-VOHR, AH-blah mahs LEHN-toh

I don't understand.
No entiendo.
Noh ehn-tee-EHN-doh

Can you say that more clearly?
¿Puedes decir eso de forma más clara?
PWEH-dehs deh-SEER EH-soh deh FOHR-mah mahs KLAH-rah

I don't speak Spanish very well.
No hablo el español muy bien.
Noh AH-bloh ehl ehs-pah-NYOHL MOO-ee bee-EHN

Can you please translate that to English for me?
¿Puedes traducirme eso al inglés, por favor?
PWEH-dehs trah-doo-SEER-meh EH-soh ahl een-GLEHS, pohr fah-VOHR

Let's talk over there where it is quieter.
Hablemos allá, donde es más silencioso.
Ah-BLEH-mohs ah-YAH, DOHN-deh ehs mahs see-lehn-see-OH-soh

Sit down over there.
Siéntate por allí.
See-EHN-tah-teh pohr ah-YEE

May I?
¿Puedo?
PWEH-doh

I am from America.
Soy de América.
SOH-ee deh ah-MEH-ree-kah

Am I talking too much?
¿Estoy hablando demasiado?
Ehs-TOH-ee ah-BLAHN-doh deh-mah-see-AH-doh

I speak your language badly.
Hablo mal tu idioma.
AH-bloh mahl too ee-dee-OH-mah

Am I saying that word correctly?
¿Estoy diciendo bien esa palabra?
Ehs-TOH-ee dee-see-EHN-doh bee-EHN EH-sah pah-LAH-brah

You speak English very well.
Tú hablas muy bien el inglés.
Too AH-blahs MOO-ee bee-EHN ehl een-GLEHS

This is my first time in your lovely country.
Es la primera vez que visito tu hermoso país.
Ehs lah pree-MEH-rah vehs keh vee-SEE-toh too ehr-MOH-soh pah-EES

Write that information down on this piece of paper.
Escribe esa información en este pedazo de papel.
Ehs-KREE-beh EH-sah een-fohr-mah-see-OHN ehn EHS-teh peh-DAH-soh deh pah-PEHL

Do you understand?
¿Entiendes?
Ehn-tee-EHN-dehs

How do you pronounce that word?
¿Cómo pronuncias esa palabra?
KOH-moh proh-NOON-see-ahs EH-sah pah-LAH-brah

Is this how you write this word?
¿Así es como se escribe esta palabra?
Ah-SEE ehs KOH-moh seh ehs-KREE-beh EHS-tah pah-LAH-brah

Can you give me an example?
¿Puedes darme un ejemplo?
PWEH-dehs DAHR-meh oon eh-HEHM-ploh

Wait a moment, please.
Espera un momento, por favor.
Ehs-PEH-rah oon moh-MEHN-toh, pohr fah-VOHR

If there is anything you want, tell me.
Si hay algo que quieras, dime.
See AH-ee AHL-goh keh kee-EH-rahs, DEE-meh

I don't want to bother you anymore, so I will go.
No quiero molestarte más, así que me iré.
Noh kee-EH-roh moh-lehs-TAHR-teh mahs, ah-SEE keh meh ee-REH

Please take care of yourself.
Por favor, cuídate.
Pohr fah-VOHR, koo-EE-dah-teh

When you arrive, let us know.
Avísanos cuando llegues.
Ah-VEE-sah-nohs KWAHN-doh YEH-gehs

DATE NIGHT

What is your telephone number?
¿Cuál es tu número de teléfono?
Kwahl ehs too NOO-meh-roh deh teh-LEH-foh-noh

I'll call you for the next date.
Te llamaré para la próxima cita.
Teh yah-mah-REH PAH-rah lah PROHK-see-mah SEE-tah

I had a good time, can't wait to see you again.
La pasé excelente, ya quiero verte otra vez.
Lah pah-SEH ehk-seh-LEHN-teh, yah kee-EH-roh VEHR-teh OH-trah vehs

I'll pay for dinner tonight.
Yo pagaré la cena esta noche.
Yoh pah-gah-REH lah SEH-nah EHS-tah NOH-cheh

Dinner at my place?
¿Quieres cenar en mi casa?
Kee-EH-rehs seh-NAHR ehn mee KAH-sah

I don't think we should see each other anymore.
Creo que no debemos vernos más.
KREH-oh keh noh deh-behmohs VEHR-nohs mahs

I'm afraid this will be the last time we see each other.
Temo que esta será la última vez que nos veamos.
TEH-moh keh EHS-tah seh-RAH lah OOL-tee-mah vehs keh nohs veh-AH-mohs

You look fantastic.
Te ves fantástica.
Teh vehs fahn-TAHS-tee-kah

Would you like to dance with me?
¿Quisieras bailar conmigo?
Kee-see-EH-rahs bah-ee-LAHR kohn-MEE-goh

Are there any 3D cinemas in this city?
¿Hay algún cine 3D en esta ciudad?
AH-ee ahl-GOON SEE-neh trehs deh ehn EHS-tah see-oo-DAHD

We should walk along the beach.
Deberíamos caminar por la playa.
Deh-beh-REE-ah-mohs kah-mee-NAHR pohr lah PLAH-yah

I hope you like my car.
Espero que te guste mi auto.
Ehs-PEH-roh keh teh GOOS-teh mee AH-oo-toh

What movies are playing today?
¿Qué películas están en cartelera hoy?
Keh peh-LEE-koo-lahs ehs-TAHN ehn kahr-teh-LEH-rah OH-ee

I've seen this film, but I wouldn't mind watching it again.
Ya vi esta película, pero no me importaría verla otra vez.
Yah vee EHS-tah peh-LEE-koo-lah, PEH-roh noh meh eem-pohr-tah-REE-ah VEHR-lah OH-trah vehs

Do you know how to dance to salsa?
¿Sabes bailar salsa?
SAH-behs bah-ee-LAHR SAHL-sah

We can dance all night.
Podemos bailar toda la noche.
Poh-DEH-mohs bah-ee-LAHR TOH-dah lah NOH-cheh

I have some friends that will be joining us tonight.
Tengo unos amigos que vendrán con nosotros esta noche.
TEHN-goh OO-nohs ah-MEE-gohs keh vehn-DRAHN kohn noh-SOH-trohs EHS-tah NOH-cheh

Is this a musical or a regular concert?
¿Este es un musical o un concierto regular?
EHS-teh ehs oon moo-see-KAHL oh oon kohn-see-EHR-toh rreh-goo-LAHR

Did you get VIP tickets?
¿Tienes entradas VIP?
Tee-EH-nehs ehn-TRAH-dahs VIP

I'm going to have to cancel on you tonight. Maybe another time?
Tendré que cancelar nuestra cita de esta noche. ¿Puede ser otro día?

Tehn-DREH keh kahn-seh-LAHR NWEHS-trah SEE-tah deh EHS-tah NOH-cheh. PWEH-deh sehr OH-troh DEE-ah

If you want, we can go to your place.
Si quieres, podemos ir a tu casa.
See kee-EH-rehs, poh-DEH-mohs eer ah too KAH-sah

I'll pick you up tonight.
Te recogeré en la noche.
Teh rreh-koh-heh-REH ehn lah NOH-cheh

This one is for you!
¡Este es para ti!
EHS-teh ehs PAH-rah tee

What time does the party start?
¿A qué hora comienza la fiesta?
Ah keh OH-rah koh-mee-EHN-sah lah fee-EHS-tah

Will it end on time or will you have to leave early?
¿Terminará a tiempo o tendrás que irte antes?
Tehr-mee-nah-RAH ah tee-EHM-poh oh tehn-DRAHS keh EER-teh AHN-tehs

Did you like your gift?
¿Te gustó tu regalo?
Teh goos-TOH too rreh-GAH-loh

I want to invite you to watch a movie with me tonight.
Quiero invitarte a ver una película conmigo esta noche.
Kee-EH-roh een-vee-TAHR-teh ah vehr OO-nah peh-LEE-koo-lah kohn-MEE-goh EHS-tah NOH-cheh

Do you want anything to drink?
¿Quieres algo de beber?
Kee-EH-rehs AHL-goh deh beh-BEHR

I am twenty-six years old.
Tengo veintiséis años.
TEHN-goh veh-een-tee-SEH-ees AH-nyohs

You're invited to a small party I'm having at my house.
Te invito a una pequeña fiesta que tendré en mi casa.
Teh een-VEE-toh ah OO-nah peh-KEH-nyah fee-EHS-tah keh tehn-DREH
ehn mee KAH-sah

I love you.
Te amo.
Teh AH-moh

We should go to the arcade.
Deberíamos ir a la sala de juegos.
Deh-beh-REE-ah-mohs eer ah lah SAH-lah deh hoo-EH-gohs

Have you ever played this game before?
¿Has jugado este juego antes?
Ahs hoo-GAH-doh EHS-teh hoo-EH-goh AHN-tehs

Going on this ferry would be really romantic.
Un paseo en este ferri sería muy romántico.
Oon pah-SEH-oh ehn EHS-teh FEH-rree seh-REE-ah MOO-ee rroh-MAHN-
tee-koh

How about a candlelight dinner?
¿Qué tal una cena a la luz de las velas?
Keh tahl OO-nah SEH-nah ah lah loos deh lahs VEH-lahs

Let's dance and sing!
¡Vamos a cantar y bailar!
VAH-mohs ah kahn-TAHR ee bah-ee-LAHR

Will you marry me?
¿Te casarías conmigo?
Teh kah-sah-REE-ahs kohn-MEE-goh

Set the table, please.
Pon la mesa, por favor.
Pohn lah MEH-sah, pohr fah-VOHR

Here are the dishes and the glasses.
Aquí están los platos y las copas.
Ah-KEE ehs-TAHN lohs PLAH-tohs ee lahs KOH-pahs

Where is the cutlery?
¿Dónde están los cubiertos?
DOHN-deh ehs-TAHN lohs koo-bee-EHR-tohs

May I hold your hand?
¿Puedo agarrar tu mano?
PWEH-doh ah-gah-RRAHR too MAH-noh

Let me get that for you.
Déjame pasarte eso.
DEH-hah-meh pah-SAHR-teh EH-soh

I think our song is playing!
Creo que nuestra canción está sonando.
KRE-oh keh NWEHS-trah kahn-see-OHN ehs-TAH soh-NAHN-doh

Let's make a wish together.
Pidamos un deseo juntos.
Pee-DAH-mohs oon deh-SEH-oh HOON-tohs

Is there anything that you want from me?
¿Hay algo que quieras de mí?
AH-ee AHL-goh keh kee-EH-rahs deh mee

There is nowhere I would rather be than right here with you.
No hay ningún lugar en el que prefiera estar más que aquí contigo.
Noh AH-ee neen-GOON loo-GAHR ehn ehl keh preh-fee-EH-rah ehs-TAHR mahs keh ah-KEE kohn-TEE-goh

I'll give you a ride back to your place.
Te llevaré de regreso a tu casa.
Teh yeh-vah-REH deh rreh-GREH-soh ah too KAH-sah

Would you like me to hold your purse?
¿Quisieras que sostenga tu bolso?
Kee-see-EH-rahs keh sohs-TEHN-gah too BOHL-soh

Let's pray before we eat our meal.
Oremos antes de comer.
Oh-REH-mohs AHN-tehs deh koh-MEHR

Do you need a napkin?
¿Necesitas una servilleta?
Neh-seh-SEE-tahs OO-nah sehr-vee-YEH-tah

I'm thirsty.
Tengo sed.
TEHN-goh sehd

I hope you enjoy your meal.
Espero que disfrutes la comida.
Ehs-PEH-roh keh dees-FROO-tehs lah koh-MEE-dah

I need to add more salt to the saltshaker.
Necesito poner más sal en el salero.
Neh-seh-SEE-toh poh-NEHR mahs sahl ehn ehl sah-LEH-roh

We should get married!
¡Deberíamos casarnos!
Deh-beh-REE-ah-mohs kah-SAHR-nohs

How old are you?
¿Cuántos años tienes?
KWAHN-tohs AH-nyohs tee-EH-nehs

Will you dream of me?
¿Soñarás conmigo?
Soh-nyah-RAHS kohn-MEE-goh

Thank you very much for the wonderful date last night.
Muchas gracias por la maravillosa cita de anoche.
GRAH-see-ahs pohr lah mah-rah-vee-YOH-sah SEE-tah deh ah-NOH-cheh

Would you like to come to a party this weekend?
¿Quisieras ir a una fiesta este fin de semana?
Kee-see-EH-rahs eer ah OO-nah fee-EHS-tah EHS-teh feen deh seh-MAH-nah

This Saturday night, right?
¿Este sábado en la noche, cierto?
EHS-teh SAH-bah-doh ehn lah NOH-cheh, see-EHR-toh

I will be lonely without you.
Me sentiré solo sin ti.
Meh sehn-tee-REH SOH-loh seen tee

Please stay the night.
Por favor, quédate esta noche
Pohr fah-VOHR, KEH-dah-teh EHS-tah NOH-cheh

I like your fragrance.
Me gusta tu perfume.
Meh GOOS-tah too pehr-FOO-meh

That is a beautiful outfit you're wearing.
Está muy bonito el atuendo que estás usando.
Ehs-TAH MOO-ee boh-NEE-toh ehl ah-too-EHN-doh keh ehs-TAHS oo-SAHN-doh

You look beautiful.
Te ves hermosa.
Teh vehs ehr-MOH-sah

Let me help you out of the car.
Déjame ayudarte a salir del auto.
DEH-hah-meh ah-yoo-DAHR-teh ah sah-LEER dehl AH-oo-toh

Sarah, will you come with me to dinner?
Sarah, ¿saldrías a cenar conmigo?
Sarah, sahl-DREE-ahs ah seh-NAHR kohn-MEE-goh

I would like to ask you out on a date.
Quisiera invitarte a salir en una cita.
Kee-see-EH-rah een-vee-TAHR-teh ah sah-LEER ehn OO-nah SEE-tah

Are you free tonight?
¿Estás libre esta noche?
Ehs-TAHS LEE-breh EHS-tah NOH-cheh

This is my phone number. Call me anytime.
Este es mi número de teléfono. Llámame cuando quieras.
EHS-teh ehs mee NOO-meh-roh deh teh-LEH-foh-noh. YAH-mah-meh KWAHN-doh kee-EH-rahs

Can I hug you?
¿Te puedo abrazar?
Teh PWEH-doh ah-brah-SAHR

Would you like to sing karaoke?
¿Quisieras cantar karaoke?
Kee-see-EH-rahs kahn-TAHR kah-rah-OH-keh

What kind of song would you like to sing?
¿Qué tipo de canción quieres cantar?
Keh TEE-poh deh kahn-see-OHN kee-EH-rehs kahn-TAHR

Have you ever sung this song before?
¿Has cantado esta canción antes?
Ahs kahn-TAH-doh EHS-tah kahn-see-OHN AHN-tehs

We can sing it together.
Podemos cantarla juntos.
Poh-DEH-mohs kahn-TAHR-lah HOON-tohs

Can I kiss you?
¿Puedo besarte?
PWEH-doh beh-SAHR-teh

Are you cold?
¿Tienes frío?
Tee-EH-nehs FREE-oh

We can stay out as late as you want.
Podemos quedarnos afuera hasta la hora que quieras.
Poh-DEH-mohs keh-DAHR-nohs ah-foo-EH-rah AHS-tah lah OH-rah keh kee-EH-rahs

Please, dinner is on me.
Por favor, yo invito la cena.
Pohr fah-VOHR, yoh een-VEE-toh lah SEH-nah

Shall we split the bill?
¿Dividimos la cuenta?
Dee-vee-DEE-mohs lah koo-EHN-tah

We should spend more time together.
Deberíamos pasar más tiempo juntos.
Deh-beh-REE-ah-mohs pah-SAHR mahs tee-EHM-poh HOON-tohs

We should walk the town tonight.
Deberíamos caminar por la ciudad esta noche.
Deh-beh-REE-ah-mohs kah-mee-NAHR pohr lah see-oo-DAHD EHS-tah NOH-cheh

Did you enjoy everything?
¿La pasaste bien?
Lah pah-SAHS-teh bee-EHN

MONEY AND SHOPPING

May I try this on?
¿Puedo probarme esto?
PWEH-doh proh-BAHR-meh EHS-toh

How much does this cost?
¿Cuánto cuesta esto?
KWAHN-toh KWEHS-tah EHS-toh

Do I sign here or here?
¿Firmo aquí o aquí?
FEER-moh ah-KEE o ah-KEE

Is that your final price?
¿Ese es su mejor precio?
¿EH-seh ehs soo meh-HOHR PREH-see-oh?

Where do I find toiletries?
¿Dónde encuentro artículos de aseo?
DOHN-deh ehn-koo-EHN-troh ahr-TEE-koo-lohs deh ah-SEH-oh

Would you be willing to take five dollars for this item?
¿Aceptarías cinco dólares por este artículo?
Ah-sehp-tah-REE-ahs SEEN-koh DOH-lah-rehs pohr EHS-teh ahr-TEE-koo-loh

I can't afford it at that price.
No puedo pagarlo a ese precio.
Noh PWEH-doh pah-GAHR-loh ah EH-seh PREH-see-oh

I can find this cheaper somewhere else.
Puedo encontrar esto más barato en otro lugar.
PWEH-doh ehn-kohn-TRAHR EHS-toh mahs bah-RAH-toh ehn OH-troh loo-GAHR

Is there a way we can haggle on price?
¿Hay alguna forma en que podamos negociar el precio?
AH-ee ahl-GOO-nah FOHR-mah ehn keh poh-DAH-mohs neh-goh-see-
AHR ehl PREH-see-oh

How many of these have you sold today?
¿Cuántos de estos han vendido hoy?
KWAHN-tohs deh EHS-tohs ahn vehn-DEE-doh OH-ee

Can you wrap that up as a gift?
¿Puedes envolverlo para un regalo?
PWEH-dehs ehn-vohl-VEHR-loh PAH-rah oon rreh-GAH-loh

Do you provide personalized letters?
¿Hacen cartas personalizadas?
AH-sehn KAHR-tahs pehr-soh-nah-lee-SAH-das

I would like this to be specially delivered to my hotel.
Me gustaría comprar esto con entrega especial a mi hotel.
Meh goos-tah-REE-ah kohm-PRAHR EHS-toh kohn ehn-TREH-gah ehs-
peh-see-AHL ah mee oh-TEHL

Can you help me, please?
¿Puedes ayudarme, por favor?
PWEH-dehs ah-yoo-DAHR-meh, pohr fah-VOHR

We should go shopping at the market.
Deberíamos ir de compras al mercado
Deh-beh-REE-ah-mohs eer deh KOHM-prahs ahl mehr-KAH-doh

Are you keeping track of the clothes that fit me?
¿Estás siguiendo cuáles prendas me quedan bien?
Ehs-TAHS see-gee-EHN-doh KWAH-lehs PREHN-dahs meh KEH-dahn bee-
EHN

Can I have one size up?
¿Me lo puedes traer en una talla más grande?
Meh loh PWEH-dehs trah-EHR ehn OO-nah TAH-yah mahs GRAHN-deh

How many bathrooms does the apartment have?
¿Cuántos baños tiene el apartamento?
KWAHN-tohs BAH-nyohs tee-EH-neh ehl ah-pahr-tah-MEHN-toh

Where's the kitchen?
¿Dónde está la cocina?
DOHN-deh ehs-TAH lah koh-SEE-nah

Does this apartment have a gas or electric stove?
¿La estufa de este apartamento es a gas o eléctrica?
Lah ehs-TOO-fah deh EHS-teh ah-pahr-tah-MEHN-toh ehs ah gahs oh eh-LEHK-tree-kah

Is there a spacious backyard?
¿Tiene un patio grande?
Tee-EH-neh oon PAH-tee-oh GRAHN-deh

How much is the down payment?
¿Cuánto es el pago inicial?
KWAHN-toh ehs ehl PAH-goh ee-nee-see-AHL

I'm looking for a furnished apartment.
Estoy buscando un apartamento amoblado.
Ehs-TOH-ee boos-KAHN-doh oon ah-pahr-tah-MEHN-toh ah-moh-BLAH-doh

I need a two-bedroom apartment to rent.
Necesito rentar un apartamento de dos habitaciones.
Neh-seh-SEE-toh rrehn-TAHR oon ah-pahr-tah-MEHN-toh deh dohs ah-bee-tah-see-OH-nehs

I'm looking for an apartment with utilities paid.
Estoy buscando un apartamento con los servicios públicos pagos.
Ehs-TOH-ee boos-KAHN-doh oon ah-pahr-tah-MEHN-toh kohn lohs sehr-VEE-see-ohs POO-blee-kohs PAH-gohs

The carpet in this apartment needs to be pulled up.
Hay que quitar la alfombra de este apartamento.
AH-ee keh kee-TAHR lah ahl-FOHM-brah deh EHS-teh ah-pahr-tah-MEHN-toh

I need you to come down on the price of this apartment.
Necesito un precio más bajo para este apartamento.
Neh-seh-SEE-toh oon PREH-see-oh mahs BAH-hoh PAH-rah EHS-teh ah-pahr-tah-MEHN-toh

Will I be sharing this place with other people?
¿Estaré compartiendo este apartamento con otras personas?
Ehs-tah-REH kohm-pahr-tee-EHN-doh EHS-teh ah-pahr-tah-MEHN-toh
kohn OH-trahs pehr-SOH-nahs

How do you work the fireplace?
¿Cómo funciona la chimenea?
KOH-moh foon-see-OH-nah lah chee-meh-NEH-ah

Are there any curfew rules attached to this apartment?
¿Hay reglas sobre las horas de llegada en este apartamento?
AH-ee RREH-glahs SOH-breh lahs OH-rahs deh yeh-GAH-dah ehn EHS-
teh ah-pahr-tah-MEHN-toh

How long is the lease for this place?
¿Cuánto dura el contrato de arrendamiento de este lugar?
KWAHN-toh DOO-rah ehl kohn-TRAH-toh deh ah-rrehn-dah-mee-EHN-
toh deh EHS-teh loo-GAHR

Do you gamble?
¿Tú apuestas?
Too ah-PWEHS-tahs

We should go to a casino.
Deberíamos ir a un casino
Deh-beh-REE-ah-mohs eer ah oon kah-SEE-noh

There is really good horse racing in this area.
Las carreras de caballos son muy buenas en esta área.
Lahs kah-RREH-rahs deh kah-BAH-yohs sohn MOO-ee BWEH-nahs ehn
EHS-tah AH-reh-ah

Do you have your ID so that we can go gambling?
¿Tienes tu tarjeta de identificación para que podamos ir a apostar?
Tee-EH-nehs too tahr-HEH-tah deh ee-dehn-tee-fee-kah-see-OHN PAH-
rah keh poh-DAH-mohs eer ah ah-pohs-TAHR

Who did you bet on?
¿A quién le apostaste?
Ah kee-EHN leh ah-pohs-TAHS-teh

I am calling about the apartment that you placed in the ad.
Estoy llamando por el apartamento del anuncio.
Ehs-TOH-ee yah-MAHN-doh pohr ehl ah-pahr-tah-MEHN-toh dehl ah-NOON-see-oh

How much did you bet?
¿Cuánto apostaste?
KWAHN-toh ah-pohs-TAHS-teh

We should go running with the bulls!
¡Deberíamos ir a correr con los toros!
Deh-beh-REE-ah-mohs eer ah koh-RREHR kohn lohs TOH-rohs

Is Adele coming to sing at this venue tonight?
¿Adele vendrá a cantar en este lugar esta noche?
Adele vehn-DRAH ah kahn-TAHR ehn EHS-teh loo-GAHR EHS-tah NOH-cheh

How much is the item you have in the window?
¿Cuánto cuesta el artículo que está en la vitrina?
KWAHN-toh KWEHS-tah ehl ahr-TEE-koo-loh keh ehs-TAH ehn lah vee-TREE-nah

Do you have payment plans?
¿Tienes planes de financiación?
Tee-EH-nehs PLAH-nehs deh fee-nahn-see-ah-see-OHN

Do these two items come together?
¿Estos dos productos vienen juntos?
EHS-tohs dohs proh-DOOK-tohs vee-EH-nehn HOON-tohs

Are these parts cheaply made?
¿Estas partes son de mala calidad?
EHS-tahs PAHR-tehs sohn deh MAH-lah kah-lee-DAHD

This is a huge bargain!
¡Esta es una ganga!
EHS-tah ehs OO-nah GAHN-gah

I like this. How does three hundred dollars sound?
Me gusta esto. ¿Qué tal suenan trescientos dólares?
Meh GOOS-tah EHS-toh. Keh tahl soo-EH-nahn treh-see-EHN-tohs DOH-lah-rehs

Two hundred is all I can offer. That is my final price.
Doscientos es todo lo que puedo ofrecer. Esa es mi oferta final.
Doh-see-EHN-tohs ehs TOH-doh loh keh PWEH-doh oh-freh-SEHR. EH-sah ehs mee oh-FEHR-tah fee-NAHL

Do you have cheaper versions of this item?
¿Tienes alguna versión más económica de este producto?
Tee-EH-nehs ahl-GOO-nah vehr-see-OHN mahs eh-koh-NOH-mee-kah deh EHS-teh proh-DOOK-toh

Do you have the same item with a different pattern?
¿Tienes este mismo producto con un patrón diferente?
Tee-EH-nehs EHS-teh MEES-moh proh-DOOK-toh kohn oon pah-TROHN dee-feh-REHN-teh

How much is this worth?
¿Cuánto vale esto?
KWAHN-toh VAH-leh EHS-toh

Can you pack this up and send it to my address on file?
¿Puedes envolver esto y enviarlo a mi dirección?
PWEH-dehs ehn-vohl-VEHR EHS-toh ee ehn-vee-AHR-loh ah mee dee-rehk-see-OHN

Does it fit?
¿Sí me queda?
See meh KEH-dah

They are too big for me.
Están muy grandes para mí.
Ehs-TAHN MOO-ee GRAHN-dehs PAH-rah mee

Please find me another but in the same size.
Por favor, tráeme otro, pero en la misma talla.
Pohr fah-VOHR, TRAH-eh-meh OH-troh, PEH-roh ehn la MEES-mah TAH-yah

It fits but is tight around my waist.
Me queda, pero está muy ajustado en la cintura.
Meh KEH-dah, PEH-roh ehs-TAH MOO-ee ah-hoos-TAH-doh ehn lah seen-TOO-rah

Can I have one size down?
¿Me trae una talla menos?
Meh TRAH-eh OO-nah TAH-yah MEH-nohs

Size twenty, American.
Talla veinte, americana.
TAH-yah VEH-een-teh, ah-meh-ree-KAH-nah

Do you sell appliances for the home?
¿Venden electrodomésticos para el hogar?
VEHN-dehn eh-lehk-troh-doh-MEHS-tee-kohs PAH-rah ehl oh-GAHR

Not now, thank you.
Ahora no, gracias.
Ah-OH-rah noh. GRAH-see-ahs

I'm looking for something special.
Estoy buscando un detalle especial.
Ehs-TOH-ee boos-KAHN-doh oon deh-TAH-yeh ehs-peh-see-AHL

I'll call you when I need you.
Te llamaré cuando te necesite.
Teh yah-mah-REH KWAHN-doh teh neh-seh-SEE-teh

Do you have this in my size?
¿Tienes esto en mi talla?
Tee-EH-nehs EHS-toh ehn mee TAH-yah

On which floor can I find cologne?
¿En qué piso puedo encontrar los perfumes?
Ehn keh PEE-soh PWEH-doh ehn-kohn-TRAHR lohs pehr-FOO-mehs

Where is the entrance?
¿Dónde está la entrada?
DOHN-deh ehs-TAH lah ehn-TRAH-dah

Do I exit from that door?
¿Salgo por esa puerta?
SAHL-goh pohr EH-sah PWEHR-tah

Where is the elevator?
¿Dónde está el elevador?
DOHN-deh ehs-TAH ehl eh-leh-vah-DOHR

Do I push or pull to get this door open?
¿Halo o empujo para abrir esta puerta?
AH-loh oh ehm-POO-hoh PAH-rah ah-BREER EHS-tah PWEHR-tah

I already have that, thanks.
Ya lo tengo, gracias.
Yah loh TEHN-goh, GRAH-see-ahs

Where can I try this on?
¿Dónde me puedo probar esto?
DOHN-deh meh PWEH-doh proh-BAHR EHS-toh

This mattress is very soft.
Este colchón es muy suave.
EHS-teh kohl-CHOHN ehs MOO-ee soo-AH-veh

What is a good place for birthday gifts?
¿Dónde puedo conseguir regalos de cumpleaños?
DOHN-deh PWEH-doh kohn-seh-GEER rreh-GAH-lohs deh koom-pleh-AH-nyos

I'm just looking but thank you.
Solo estoy mirando, gracias.
SOH-loh ehs-TOH-ee mee-RAHN-doh, GRAH-see-ahs

Yes, I will call you when I need you, thank you.
Sí, te llamaré cuando te necesite, gracias.
See, teh yah-mah-REH KWAHN-doh teh neh-seh-SEE-teh, GRAH-see-ahs

Do you accept returns?
¿Aceptas devoluciones?
Ah-SEHP-tahs deh-voh-loo-see-OH-nehs

Here is my card and receipt for the return.
Aquí están mi tarjeta y la factura para la devolución.
Ah-KEE ehs-TAHN mee tahr-HEH-tah ee lah fahk-TOO-rah PAH-rah lah deh-voh-loo-see-OHN

Where are the lady's clothes?
¿Dónde está la sección de ropa para mujeres?
DOHN-deh ehs-TAH lah sehk-see-OHN deh ROH-pah PAH-rah moo-HEH-rehs

What sizes are available for this item?
¿En qué tallas tienes disponible este artículo?
Ehn keh TAH-yahs tee-EH-nehs dees-poh-NEE-bleh EHS-teh ahr-TEE-koo-loh

Is there an ATM machine nearby?
¿Hay algún cajero automático por aquí?
AH-ee ahl-GOON kah-HEH-roh ah-oo-toh-MAH-tee-koh pohr ah-KEE

What forms of payment do you accept? (REPETITIVE)
¿Qué medios de pagos aceptan?
Keh MEH-dee-ohs deh PAH-goh ah-SEHP-tahn

That doesn't interest me.
Eso no me interesa.
EH-soh noh meh een-teh-REH-sah

I don't like it, but thank you.
No me gusta, pero gracias.
Noh meh GOOS-tah, PEH-roh GRAH-see-ahs

Do you take American dollars?
¿Aceptan dólares americanos?
Ah-SEHP-tahn DOH-lah-rehs ah-meh-ree-KAH-nohs

Can you make change for me?
¿Puedes cambiarme este billete?
PWEH-dehs kahm-bee-AHR-meh EHS-teh bee-YEH-teh

What is the closest place to get change for my money?
¿Cuál es el lugar más cercano para cambiar este billete?
Kwahl ehs ehl loo-GAHR mahs sehr-KAH-noh PAH-rah kahm-bee-AHR EHS-teh bee-YEH-teh

Are travelers checks able to be changed here?
¿Aquí se pueden cambiar los cheques extranjeros?
Ah-KEE seh PWEH-dehn kahm-bee-AHR lohs CHEH-kehs ehks-trahn-HEH-rohs

What is the current exchange rate?
¿Cuál es la tasa de cambio actual?
Kwahl ehs lah TAH-sah deh KAHM-bee-oh ahk-too-AHL

What is the closest place to exchange money?
¿Cuál es el lugar más cercano para cambiar dinero?
Kwahl ehs ehl loo-GAHR mahs sehr-KAH-noh PAH-rah kahm-bee-AHR
dee-NEH-roh

Do you need to borrow money? How much?
¿Necesitas dinero prestado? ¿Cuánto?
Neh-seh-SEE-tahs dee-NEH-roh prehs-TAH-doh. KWAHN-toh

Can this bank exchange my money?
¿Este banco puede cambiar mi dinero?
EHS-teh BAHN-koh PWEH-deh kahm-bee-AHR mee dee-NEH-roh

What is the exchange rate for the American dollar?
¿Cuál es la tasa de cambio para el dólar americano?
Kwahl ehs lah TAH-sah deh KAHM-bee-oh PAH-rah ehl DOH-lahr ah-
meh-ree-KAH-noh

Will you please exchange me fifty dollars?
¿Me cambiarías quince dólares, por favor?
Meh kahm-bee-ah-REE-ahs KEEN-seh DOH-lah-rehs, pohr fah-VOHR

I would like a receipt with that.
Quisiera un recibo con eso.
Kee-see-EH-rah oon rreh-SEE-boh kohn EH-soh

Your commission rate is too high.
Su tasa de comisión es muy alta.
Soo TAH-sah deh koh-mee-see-OHN ehs MOO-ee AHL-tah

Does this bank have a lower commission rate?
¿Este banco tiene una tasa de comisión más baja?
EHS-teh BAHN-koh tee-EH-neh OO-nah TAH-sah deh koh-mee-see-OHN
mahs BAH-hah

Do you take cash?
¿Aceptas efectivo?
Ah-SEHP-tahs eh-fehk-TEE-voh

Where can I exchange dollars?
¿Dónde puedo cambiar dólares?
DOHN-deh PWEH-doh kahm-bee-AHR DOH-lah-rehs

I want to exchange dollars for yen.
Quiero cambiar dólares por yenes.
Kee-EH-roh kahm-bee-AHR DOH-lah-rehs pohr YEH-nehs

Do you take credit cards?
¿Aceptas tarjetas de crédito?
Ah-SEHP-tahs tahr-HEH-tahs deh KREH-dee-toh

Here is my credit card.
Aquí está mi tarjeta de crédito.
Ah-KEE ehs-TAH mee tahr-HEH-tah deh KREH-dee-toh

One moment, let me check the receipt.
Un momento, déjame revisar el recibo.
Oon moh-MEHN-toh, DEH-hah-meh rreh-vee-SAHR ehl reh-SEE-boh

Do I need to pay tax?
¿Tengo que pagar un impuesto?
TEHN-goh keh pah-GAHR oon eem-PWEHS-toh

How much is this item with tax?
¿Cuánto cuesta este artículo con impuestos incluidos?
KWAHN-toh KWEHS-tah EHS-teh ahr-TEE-koo-loh kohn eem-PWEHS-tohs een-kloo-EE-dohs

Where is the cashier?
¿Dónde está el cajero?
DOHN-deh ehs-TAH ehl kah-HEH-roh

Excuse me, I'm looking for a dress.
Disculpa, estoy buscando un vestido.
Dees-KOOL-pah, ehs-TOH-ee boos-KAHN-doh oon vehs-TEE-doh

That's a lot for that dress.
Es mucho dinero por ese vestido.
Ehs MOO-choh dee-NEH-roh pohr EH-seh vehs-TEE-doh

Sorry, but I don't want it.
Disculpa, pero no lo quiero.
Dees-KOOL-pah, PEH-roh noh loh kee-EH-roh

Okay I will take it.
Ok, lo llevaré.
Ok, loh yeh-vah-REH

I'm not interested if you are going to sell it at that price.
No me interesa si vas a venderlo a ese precio.
Noh meh een-teh-REH-sah see vahs ah vehn-DEHR-loh ah EH-seh PREH-see-oh

You are cheating me at the current price.
Estás abusando con el precio actual.
Ehs-TAHS ah-boo-SAHN-doh kohn ehl PREH-see-oh ahk-too-AHL

No thanks. I'll only take it if you lower the price by half.
No, gracias. Solo lo llevaré si bajas el precio a la mitad.
Noh, GRAH-see-ahs. SOH-loh loh yeh-vah-REH see BAH-HAHS ehl PREH-see-oh ah lah mee-TAHD

That is a good price, I'll take it.
Ese es un buen precio, me lo llevaré.
EH-seh ehs oon bwehn PREH-see-oh, meh loh yeh-vah-REH

Do you sell souvenirs for tourists?
¿Venden souvenirs para los turistas?
VEHN-dehn souvenirs PAH-rah lohs too-REES-tahs

Can I have a bag with that?
¿Me regalas una bolsa con eso?
Meh rreh-GAH-lahs OO-nah BOHL-sah kohn EH-soh

Is this the best bookstore in the city?
¿Esta es la mejor librería de la ciudad?
EHS-tah ehs lah meh-HOHR lee-breh-REE-ah deh lah see-oo-DAHD

I would like to go to a game shop to buy comic books.
Me gustaría ir a una tienda de juegos a comprar un libro de historietas.
Meh goos-tah-REE-ah eer ah OO-nah tee-EHN-dah deh hoo-EH-gohs ah kohm-PRAHR oon LEE-broh deh ees-toh-ree-EH-tahs

Are you able to ship my products overseas?
¿Pueden enviar mis productos al extranjero?
PWEH-dehn ehn-vee-AHR mees proh-DOOK-tohs ahl ehks-trahn-HEH-roh

CHILDREN AND PETS

Which classroom does my child attend?
¿En qué salón está mi hijo?
Ehn keh sah-LOHN ehs-TAH mee EE-hoh

Is the report due before the weekend?
¿El informe debe entregarse antes del fin de semana?
Ehl een-FOHR-meh DEH-beh ehn-treh-GAHR-seh AHN-tehs dehl feen deh seh-MAH-nah

I'm waiting for my mom to pick me up.
Estoy esperando que mi mamá venga a recogerme.

Ehs-TOH-ee ehs-peh-RAHN-doh keh mee mah-MAH VEHN-gah ah rreh-koh-HEHR-meh

What time does the school bus run?
¿A qué hora pasa el bus escolar?
Ah keh OH-rah PAH-sah ehl boos ehs-koh-LAHR

I need to see the principal.
Necesito ver al director.
Neh-seh-SEE-toh vehr ahl dee-rehk-TOHR

I would like to report bullying.
Quisiera reportar un caso de acoso.
Kee-see-EH-rah rreh-pohr-TAHR oon KAH-soh deh ah-KOH-soh

What are the leash laws in this area?
¿Cuáles son las leyes sobre llevar a las mascotas con correa en esta área?
KWAH-lehs sohn lahs LEH-yehs SOH-breh yeh-VAHR ah lahs mahs-KOH-tahs kohn koh-RREH-ah ehn EHS-tah AH-reh-ah

Please keep your dog away from mine.
Por favor, que tu perro no se acerque al mío.
Pohr fah-VOHR, keh too PEH-rroh noh seh ah-SEHR-keh ahl MEE-oh

112

My dog doesn't bite.
Mi perro no muerde.
Mee PEH-rroh noh moo-EHR-deh

I am allergic to cat hair.
Soy alérgico al pelo de gato.
SOH-ee ah-LEHR-hee-koh ahl PEH-loh deh GAH-toh

Don't leave the door open or the cat will run out!
¡No dejes la puerta abierta o se saldrá el gato!
Noh DEH-hehs lah PWEHR-tah ah-bee-EHR-tah oh seh sahl-DRAH ehl
GAH-toh

Have you fed the dogs yet?
¿Ya alimentaste a los perros?
Yah ah-lee-mehn-TAHS-teh ah lohs PEH-rrohs

We need to take the dog to the veterinarian.
Tenemos que llevar al perro a la veterinaria.
Teh-NEH-mohs keh yeh-VAHR ahl PEH-rroh ah lah veh-teh-ree-NAH-ree-
ah

Are there any open roster spots on the team?
¿Hay alguna posición disponible en el equipo?
AH-ee ahl-GOO-nah poh-see-see-OHN dees-poh-NEE-bleh ehn ehl eh-
KEE-poh

My dog is depressed.
Mi perro está deprimido.
Mee PEH-rroh ehs-TAH deh-pree-MEE-doh

Don't feed the dog table scraps.
No alimentes al perro con las sobras.
Noh ah-lee-MEHN-tehs ahl PEH-rroh kohn lahs SOH-brahs

Don't let the cat climb up on the furniture.
No dejes que el gato se suba a los muebles.
Noh DEH-hehs keh ehl GAH-toh seh SOO-bah ah lohs moo-EH-blehs

The dog is not allowed to sleep in the bed with you.
El perro no puede dormir en la cama contigo.
Ehl PEH-rroh noh PWEH-deh dohr-MEER ehn lah KAH-mah kohn-TEE-goh

There is dog poop on the floor. Clean it up.
Hay caca de perro en el suelo. Límpialo.
AH-ee KAH-kah deh PEH-rroh ehn ehl soo-EH-loh. LEEM-pee-ah-loh

When was the last time you took the dog for a walk?
¿Cuándo fue la última vez que sacaste al perro a pasear?
KWAHN-doh foo-EH lah OOL-tee-mah vehs keh sah-KAHS-teh ahl PEH-rroh ah pah-seh-AHR

Are you an international student? How long are you attending?
¿Eres un estudiante internacional? ¿Cuánto tiempo vas a estar aquí?
EH-rehs oon ehs-too-dee-AHN-teh een-tehr-nah-see-oh-NAHL. KWAHN-toh tee-EHM-poh vahs ah ehs-TAHR ah-KEE

Are you a French student?
¿Eres un estudiante francés?
EH-rehs oon ehs-too-dee-AHN-teh frahn-SEHS

I am an American student that is here for the semester.
Soy un estudiante americano que está aquí por este semestre.
SOH-ee oon ehs-too-dee-AHN-teh ah-meh-ree-KAH-noh keh ehs-TAH ah-KEE pohr EHS-teh seh-MEHS-treh

Please memorize this information.
Por favor, memoriza esta información.
Pohr fah-VOHR, meh-moh-REE-sah EHS-tah een-fohr-mah-see-OHN

This is my roommate Max.
Este es mi compañero de habitación, Max.
EHS-teh ehs mee kohm-pah-NYEH-roh deh ah-bee-tah-see-OHN, Max.

Are these questions likely to appear on the exam?
¿Estas preguntas podrían aparecer en el examen?
EHS-tahs preh-GOON-tahs poh-DREE-ahn ah-pah-reh-SEHR ehn ehl ehk-SAH-mehn

Teacher, say that once more please.
Maestro, por favor, repita eso.
Mah-EHS-troh, pohr fah-VOHR, rreh-PEE-tah EH-soh

I didn't do well on the quiz.
No me fue bien en el quiz.
Noh meh foo-EH bee-EHN ehn ehl quiz

Go play outside but stay where I can see you.
Juega afuera, pero quédate donde yo pueda verte.
Hoo-EH-gah ah-foo-EH-rah, PEH-roh KEH-dah-teh DOHN-deh yoh PWEH-dah VEHR-teh

How is your daughter?
¿Cómo está tu hija?
KOH-moh ehs-TAH too EE-hah

I'm going to walk the dogs.
Voy a pasear a los perros.
VOH-ee ah pah-seh-AHR ah lohs PEH-rrohs

She's not very happy here.
Ella no es muy feliz aquí.
EH-yah noh ehs MOO-ee feh-LEES ah-KEE

I passed the quiz with high marks!
¡Pasé el quiz con una calificación alta!
Pah-SEH ehl quiz kohn OO-nah kah-lee-fee-kah-see-OHN AHL-tah

What program are you enrolled in?
¿En qué programa estás inscrito?
Ehn keh proh-GRAH-mah ehs-TAHS eens-KREE-toh

I really like my English teacher.
Me gusta mucho mi profesor de inglés.
Meh GOOS-tah MOO-choh mee proh-feh-SOHR deh een-GLEHS

I have too much homework to do.
Tengo mucha tarea en casa por hacer.
TEHN-goh MOO-chah tah-REH-ah ehn KAH-sah pohr ah-SEHR

Tomorrow, I have to take my dog to the vet.
Tengo que llevar a mi perro al veterinario mañana.
TEHN-goh keh yeh-VAHR ah mee PEH-rroh ahl veh-teh-ree-NAH-ree-oh mah-NYAH-nah

When do we get to go to lunch?
¿Cuándo podemos salir a almorzar?
KWAHN-doh poh-DEH-mohs sah-LEER ah ahl-mohr-SAHR

My dog swallowed something he shouldn't have.
Mi perro se tragó algo que no debía.
Mee PEH-rroh seh trah-GOH AHL-goh keh noh deh-BEE-ah

We need more toys for our dog to play with.
Necesitamos más juguetes para que nuestro perro juegue.
Neh-seh-see-TAH-mohs mahs hoo-GEH-tehs PAH-rah keh NWEHS-troh
PEH-rroh hoo-EH-geh

Can you please change the litter box?
¿Puedes cambiar la caja de arena, por favor?
PWEH-dehs kahm-bee-AHR lah KAH-hah deh ah-REH-nah, pohr fah-
VOHR

Get a lint brush and roll it to get the hair off your clothes.
Consigue un cepillo para pelusa y pásalo por tu ropa para quitar el pelo.
Kohn-SEE-geh oon seh-PEE-yoh PAH-rah peh-LOO-sah ee PAH-sah-loh
pohr too RROH-pah PAH-rah kee-TAHR ehl PEH-loh

Can you help me study?
¿Puedes ayudarme a estudiar?
PWEH-dehs ah-yoo-DAHR-meh ah ehs-too-dee-AHR

I have to go study in my room.
Tengo que ir a estudiar en mi habitación.
TEHN-goh keh eer ah ehs-too-dee-AHR ehn mee ah-bee-tah-see-OHN

We went to the campus party and it was a lot of fun.
Fuimos a la fiesta del campus y fue muy divertido.
Foo-EE-mohs ah lah fee-EHS-tah dehl campus ee foo-EH MOO-ee dee-
vehr-TEE-doh

Can you use that word in a sentence?
¿Puedes usar esa palabra en una oración?
PWEH-dehs oo-SAHR EH-sah pah-LAH-brah ehn OO-nah oh-rah-see-OHN

How do you spell that word?
¿Cómo deletreas esa palabra?
KOH-moh deh-leh-TREH-ahs EH-sah pah-LAH-brah

Go play with your brother.
Ve a jugar con tu hermano.
Veh ah hoo-GAHR kohn too ehr-MAH-noh

Come inside! It is dinnertime.
¡Entra! Es hora de cenar.
EHN-trah. Ehs OH-rah deh seh-NAHR

Tell me about your day.
Cuéntame cómo estuvo tu día
KWEHN-tah-meh KOH-moh ehs-TOO-voh too DEE-ah

Is there anywhere you want to go?
¿Hay algún sitio al que quieras ir?
AH-ee ahl-GOON SEE-tee-oh ahl keh kee-EH-rahs eer

How are you feeling?
¿Cómo te sientes?
KOH-moh teh see-EHN-tehs

What do you want me to make for dinner tonight?
¿Qué quieres que haga de cenar esta noche?
Keh kee-EH-rehs keh AH-gah deh seh-NAHR EHS-tah NOH-cheh

It's time for you to take a bath.
Es hora de que te bañes.
Ehs OH-rah deh keh teh BAH-nyehs

Brush your teeth and wash behind your ears.
Cepíllate los dientes y lávate detrás de las orejas.
Seh-PEE-yah-teh lohs dee-EHN-tehs ee LAH-vah-teh deh-TRAHS deh lahs
oh-REH-hahs

You're not wearing that to bed.
No vas a usar eso para ir a dormir.
Noh vahs ah oo-SAHR EH-soh PAH-rah eer ah dohr-MEER

I don't like the way you're dressed. Put something else on.
No me gusta cómo estás vestida. Ponte otra cosa.
Noh meh GOOS-tah KOH-moh ehs-TAHS vehs-TEE-dah. POHN-teh OH-
trah KOH-sah

Did you make any friends today?
¿Hiciste algunos amigos hoy?
Ee-SEES-teh ahl-GOO-nohs ah-MEE-gohs OH-ee

Let me see your homework.
Déjame ver tu tarea.
DEH-hah-meh vehr too tah-REH-ah

Do I need to call your school?
¿Necesito llamar a tu escuela?
Neh-seh-SEE-toh yah-MAHR ah too ehs-koo-EH-lah

The dog can't go outside right now.
El perro no puede salir ahora mismo.
Ehl PEH-rroh noh PWEH-deh sah-LEER ah-OH-rah MEES-moh

Is the new quiz going to be available next week?
¿El nuevo quiz estará disponible la próxima semana?
Ehl NWEH-voh quiz ehs-tah-RAH dees-poh-NEE-bleh lah PROHK-see-mah
seh-MAH-nah

Are we allowed to use calculators with the test?
¿Podemos usar calculadora durante la prueba?
Poh-DEH-mohs oo-SAHR kahl-koo-lah-DOH-rah doo-RAHN-teh lah proo-
EH-bah

I would like to lead today's lesson.
Quisiera dirigir la lección de hoy.
Kee-see-EH-rah dee-ree-HEER lah lehk-see-OHN deh OH-ee

I have a dorm curfew, so I need to go back.
Tengo un toque de queda en el dormitorio, así que necesito regresar.
TEHN-goh oon TOH-keh deh KEH-dah ehn ehl dohr-mee-TOH-ree-oh, ah-
SEE keh neh-seh-SEE-toh rreh-greh-SAHR

Do I have to use pencil or ink?
¿Tengo que usar lápiz o bolígrafo?
TEHN-goh keh oo-SAHR LAH-pees oh boh-LEE-grah-foh

Are cell phones allowed in class?
¿Los celulares están permitidos en clase?
Lohs seh-loo-LAH-rehs ehs-TAHN pehr-mee-TEE-dohs ehn KLAH-seh

Where can I find the nearest dog park?
¿Dónde puedo encontrar el parque de perros más cercano?
DOHN-deh PWEH-doh ehn-kohn-TRAHR ehl PAHR-keh deh PEH-rrohs
mahs sehr-KAH-noh

Are dogs allowed to be off their leash here?
¿Los perros pueden estar sin correa aquí?
Lohs PEH-rrohs PWEH-dehn ehs-TAHR seen koh-RREH-ah ah-KEE

Are children allowed here?
¿Se permiten niños aquí?
Seh pehr-MEE-tehn NEE-nyohs ah-KEE

I would like to set up a playdate with our children.
Me gustaría elegir un día para jugar con nuestros hijos.
Meh goos-tah-REE-ah eh-leh-HEER oon DEE-ah PAH-rah hoo-GAHR kohn
NWEHS-trohs EE-hohs

I would like to invite you to my child's birthday party.
Me gustaría invitarte a la fiesta de cumpleaños de mi hijo.
Meh goos-tah-REE-ah een-vee-TAHR-teh ah lah fee-EHS-tah deh koom-
pleh-AH-nyos deh mee EE-hoh

Did you miss your dorm curfew last night?
¿Te perdiste el toque de queda de tu dormitorio anoche?
Teh pehr-DEES-teh ehl TOH-keh deh KEH-dah deh too dohr-mee-TOH-
ree-oh ah-NOH-cheh

TRAVELER'S GUIDE

Over there is the library.
La biblioteca está allá.
Lah bee-blee-oh-TEH-kah ehs-TAH ah-YAH

Just over there.
Justo por ahí.
HOOS-toh pohr ah-EE

Yes, this way.
Sí, por aquí.
See, pohr ah-KEE

I haven't done anything wrong.
No he hecho nada malo.
Noh eh EH-choh NAH-dah MAH-loh

It was a misunderstanding.
Fue un malentendido.
Foo-EH oon mahl-ehn-tehn-DEE-doh

I am an American citizen.
Soy ciudadano americano.
SOH-ee see-oo-dah-DAH-noh ah-meh-ree-KAH-noh

We are tourists on vacation.
Somos turistas de vacaciones.
SOH-mohs too-REES-tahs deh vah-kah-see-OH-nehs

I am looking for an apartment.
Estoy buscando un apartamento.
Ehs-TOH-ee boos-KAHN-doh oon ah-pahr-tah-MEHN-toh

This is a short-term stay.
Esta es una estadía corta.
EHS-tah ehs OO-nah ehs-tah-DEE-ah KOHR-tah

I am looking for a place to rent.
Estoy buscando un lugar para rentar.
Ehs-TOH-ee boos-KAHN-doh oon loo-GAHR PAH-rah rrehn-TAHR

Where can we grab a quick bite to eat?
¿Dónde podemos encontrar algo rápido para comer?
DOHN-deh poh-DEH-mohs ehn-kohn-TRAHR AHL-goh RAH-pee-doh
PAH-rah koh-MEHR

We need the cheapest place you can find.
Necesitamos el lugar más barato que puedas encontrar.
Neh-seh-see-TAH-mohs ehl loo-GAHR mahs bah-RAH-toh keh PWEH-
dahs ehn-kohn-TRAHR

Do you have a map of the city?
¿Tienes un mapa de la ciudad?
Tee-EH-nehs oon MAH-pah deh lah see-oo-DAHD

What places do tourists usually visit when they come here?
¿Qué lugares suelen visitar los turistas cuando vienen aquí?
Keh loo-GAH-rehs soo-EH-lehn vee-see-TAHR lohs too-REES-tahs
KWAHN-doh vee-EH-nehn ah-KEE

Can you take our picture, please?
¿Puedes tomarnos una foto, por favor?
PWEH-dehs toh-MAHR-nohs OO-nah FOH-toh, pohr fah-VOHR

Do you take foreign credit cards?
¿Aceptan tarjetas de crédito internacionales?
Ah-SEHP-tahn tahr-HEH-tahs deh KREH-dee-toh een-tehr-nah-see-oh-
NAH-lehs

I would like to hire a bicycle to take us around the city.
Quisiera rentar una bicicleta para conocer la ciudad.
Kee-see-EH-rah rrehn-TAHR OO-nah bee-see-KLEH-tah PAH-rah koh-
noh-SEHR lah see-oo-DAHD

Do you mind if I take pictures here?
¿Te importa si tomo fotos aquí?
Teh eem-POHR-tah see TOH-moh FOH-tohs ah-KEE

ANSWERS

Yes, to some extent.
Sí, hasta cierto punto.
See, AHS-tah see-EHR-toh POON-toh

I'm not sure.
No estoy seguro.
Noh ehs-TOH-ee seh-GOO-roh

Yes, go head.
Sí, adelante.
See, ah-deh-LAHN-teh

Yes, just like you.
Sí, justo como tú.
See, HOOS-toh KOH-moh too

No, no problem at all.
No, no hay ningún problema.
Noh, noh AH-ee neen-GOON proh-BLEH-mah

This is a little more expensive than the other item.
Esto es un poco más costoso que el otro artículo.
EHS-toh ehs oon POH-koh mahs kohs-TOH-soh keh ehl OH-troh ahr-TEE-koo-loh

My city is small, but nice.
Mi ciudad es pequeña, pero bonita.
Mee see-oo-DAHD ehs peh-KEH-nyah, PEH-roh boh-NEE-tah

This city is quite big.
Esta ciudad es bastante grande.
EHS-tah see-oo-DAHD ehs bahs-TAHN-teh GRAHN-deh

I'm from America.
Soy de América.
SOH-ee deh ah-MEH-ree-kah

We'll wait for you.
Esperaremos por ti.
Ehs-peh-rah-REH-mohs pohr tee

I love going for walks.
Me encanta ir a pasear.
Meh ehn-KAHN-tah eer ah pah-seh-AHR

I'm a woman.
Soy una mujer.
SOH-ee OO-nah moo-HEHR

Good, I'm going to see it.
Bien, voy a verlo.
Bee-EHN, VOH-ee ah VEHR-loh

So do I.
Yo también.
Yoh tahm-bee-EHN

I'll think about it and call you tomorrow with an answer.
Lo pensaré y mañana te llamo con una respuesta.
Loh pehn-sah-REH ee mah-NYAH-nah teh YAH-moh kohn OO-nah rrehs-PWEHS-tah

I'm a parent to two children.
Soy padre de dos hijos.
SOH-ee PAH-dreh deh dohs EE-hohs

Does this place have a patio?
¿Este lugar tiene patio?
EHS-teh loo-GAHR tee-EH-neh PAH-tee-oh

No, the bathroom is vacant.
No, el baño está vacío.
Noh, ehl BAH-nyoh ehs-TAH vah-SEE-oh

I'm not old enough.
No tengo la edad suficiente.
Noh TEHN-goh lah eh-DAHD soo-fee-see-EHN-teh

No, it is very easy.
No, es muy fácil.
Noh, ehs MOO-ee FAH-seel

Understood.
Entendido.
Ehn-tehn-DEE-doh

Only if you go first.
Solo si tú vas primero.
SOH-loh see too vahs pree-MEH-roh

Yes, that is correct.
Sí, eso es correcto.
See, EH-soh ehs koh-RREHK-toh

That was the wrong answer.
Esa era la respuesta equivocada.
EH-sah EH-rah lah rrehs-PWEHS-tah eh-kee-voh-KAH-dah

We haven't decided yet.
Aún no hemos decidido.
Ah-OON noh EH-mohs deh-see-DEE-doh

We can try.
Podemos intentarlo.
Poh-DEH-mohs een-tehn-TAHR-loh

I like to read books.
Me gusta leer libros.
Meh GOOS-tah leh-EHR LEE-brohs

We can go there together.
Podemos ir allí juntos.
Poh-DEH-mohs eer ah-YEE HOON-tohs

Yes, I see.
Sí, ya veo.
See, yah VEH-oh

That looks interesting.
Eso se ve interesante.
EH-soh seh veh een-teh-reh-SAHN-teh

Me neither.
Yo tampoco.
Yoh tahm-POH-koh

It was fun.
Fue divertido.
Foo-EH dee-vehr-TEE-doh

Me too.
Yo también.
Yoh tahm-bee-EHN

Stay there.
Quédate allá.
KEH-dah-teh ah-YAH

We were worried about you.
Estábamos preocupados por ti.
Ehs-TAH-bah-mohs preh-oh-koo-PAH-dohs pohr tee

No, not really.
No, en realidad no.
Noh, ehn rreh-ah-lee-DAHD noh

Unbelievable.
Increíble.
Een-kreh-EE-bleh

No, I didn't make it in time.
No, no llegué a tiempo.
Noh, noh yeh-GEH ah tee-EHM-poh

No, you cannot.
No, no puedes.
Noh, noh PWEH-dehs

Here you go.
Aquí tienes.
Ah-KEE tee-EH-nehs

It was good.
Estuvo bien.
Ehs-TOO-voh bee-EHN

Ask my wife.
Pregúntale a mi esposa.
Preh-GOON-tah-leh ah mee ehs-POH-sah

That's up to him.
Depende de él.
Deh-PEHN-deh deh ehl

That is not allowed.
Eso no está permitido.
EH-soh noh ehs-TAH pehr-mee-TEE-doh

You can stay at my place.
Puedes quedarte en mi casa.
PWEH-dehs keh-DAHR-teh ehn mee KAH-sah

Only if you want to.
Solo si tú quieres.
SOH-loh see too kee-EH-rehs

It depends on my schedule.
Depende de mi horario.
Deh-PEHN-deh deh mee oh-RAH-ree-oh

I don't think that's possible.
No creo que eso sea posible.
Noh KREH-oh keh EH-soh SEH-ah poh-SEE-bleh

You're not bothering me.
No me molestas.
Noh meh moh-LEHS-tahs

The salesman will know.
El vendedor lo sabrá.
Ehl vehn-deh-DOHR loh sah-BRAH

I have to work.
Tengo que trabajar.
TEHN-goh keh trah-bah-HAHR

I'm late.
Estoy atrasado.
Ehs-TOH-ee ah-trah-SAH-doh

To pray.
A orar.
Ah oh-RAHR

I'll do my best.
Haré lo mejor que pueda.
Ah-REH loh meh-HOHR keh PWEH-dah

DIRECTIONS

Over here.
Por aquí.
Pohr ah-KEE

Go straight ahead.
Sigue recto.
SEE-geh RREHK-toh

Follow the straight line.
Sigue la línea recta.
SEE-geh lah LEE-neh-ah RREHK-tah

Go halfway around the circle.
Ve a la mitad de la vuelta.
Veh ah lah mee-TAHD deh lah voo-EHL-tah

It is to the left.
Es hacia la izquierda.
Ehs AH-see-ah lah ees-kee-EHR-dah

Where is the party going to be?
¿Dónde va a ser la fiesta?
DOHN-deh vah ah sehr lah fee-EHS-tah

Where is the library situated?
¿Dónde está ubicada la biblioteca?
DOHN-deh ehs-TAH oo-bee-KAH-dah lah bee-blee-oh-TEH-kah

It is to the North.
Es hacia el norte.
Ehs AH-see-ah ehl NOHR-teh

You can find it down the street.
Puedes encontrarlo al final de la calle.
PWEH-dehs ehn-kohn-TRAHR-loh ahl fee-NAHL deh lah KAH-yeh

Go into the city to get there.
Entra en la ciudad para llegar allí.
EHN-trah ehn lah see-oo-DAHD PAH-rah yeh-GAHR ah-YEE

Where are you now?
¿Dónde estás ahora?
DOHN-deh ehs-TAHS ah-OH-rah

There is a fire hydrant right in front of me.
Hay un hidrante de incendios justo frente a mí.
AH-ee oon ee-DRAHN-teh deh een-SEHN-dee-ohs HOOS-toh FREHN-teh
ah mee

Do you know a shortcut?
¿Conoces un atajo?
Koh-NOH-sehs oon ah-TAH-hoh

Where is the freeway?
¿Dónde está la autopista?
DOHN-deh ehs-TAH lah ah-oo-toh-PEES-tah

Do I need exact change for the toll?
¿Necesito el dinero exacto para el peaje?
Neh-seh-SEE-toh ehl dee-NEH-roh ehk-SAHK-toh PAH-rah ehl peh-AH-
heh

At the traffic light turn right.
En el semáforo, gira a la derecha.

Ehn ehl seh-MAH-foh-roh, HEE-rah ah lah deh-REH-chah

When you get to the intersection turn left.
Cuando llegues a la intersección, gira a la izquierda.
KWAHN-doh YEH-gehs ah lah een-tehr-sehk-see-OHN, HEE-rah ah lah
ees-kee-EHR-dah

Stay in your lane until it splits off to the right.
Permanece en tu carril hasta que se divida a la derecha.
Pehr-mah-NEH-seh ehn too kah-RREEL AHS-tah keh seh dee-VEE-dah ah
lah deh-REH-chah

Don't go onto the ramp.
No vayas sobre la rampa.
Noh VAH-yahs SOH-breh lah RRAHM-pah

You are going in the wrong direction.
Estás yendo en la dirección equivocada.
Ehs-TAHS YEHN-doh ehn lah dee-rehk-see-OHN eh-kee-voh-KAH-dah

Can you guide me to this location?
¿Puedes guiarme hacia esta ubicación?
PWEH-dehs gee-AHR-meh AH-see-ah EHS-tah oo-bee-kah-see-OHN

Stop at the crossroads.
Detente en la encrucijada.
Deh-TEHN-teh ehn lah ehn-kroo-see-HAH-dah

You missed our turn. Please turn around.
Pasaste nuestra salida. Por favor, da la vuelta.
Pah-SAHS-teh NWEHS-trah sah-LEE-dah. Pohr fah-VOHR, dah lah voo-EHL-tah

It is illegal to turn here.
Es ilegal dar la vuelta aquí.
Ehs ee-leh-GAHL dahr lah voo-EHL-tah ah-KEE

We're lost, could you help us?
Estamos perdidos, ¿podrías ayudarnos?
Ehs-TAH-mohs pehr-DEE-dohs, poh-DREE-ahs ah-yoo-DAHR-nohs

APOLOGIES

Dad, I'm sorry.
Papá, lo siento.
Pah-PAH, loh see-EHN-toh

I apologize for being late.
Me disculpo por llegar tarde.
Meh dees-KOOL-poh pohr yeh-GAHR TAHR-deh

Excuse me for not bringing money.
Perdón por no traer dinero.
Pehr-DOHN pohr noh trah-EHR dee-NEH-roh

That was my fault.
Eso fue mi culpa.
EH-soh foo-EH mee KOOL-pah

It won't happen again, I'm sorry.
No pasará de nuevo, lo siento.
Noh pah-sah-RAH deh NWEH-voh, loh see-EHN-toh

I won't break another promise.
No romperé otra promesa.
Noh rrohm-peh-REH OH-trah proh-MEH-sah

You have my word that I'll be careful.
Tienes mi palabra de que seré cuidadoso.
Tee-EH-nehs mee pah-LAH-brah deh keh seh-REH koo-ee-dah-DOH-soh

I'm sorry, I wasn't paying attention.
Lo siento, no estaba prestando atención.
Loh see-EHN-toh, noh ehs-TAH-bah prehs-TAHN-doh ah-tehn-see-OHN

I regret that. I'm so sorry.
Me arrepiento de eso. Lo siento mucho.
Meh ah-rreh-pee-EHN-toh deh EH-soh. Loh see-EHN-toh MOO-choh

I'm sorry, but today I can't.
Perdón, hoy no puedo.
Pehr-DOHN, OH-ee noh PWEH-doh

It's not your fault, I'm sorry.
No es tu culpa, yo lo siento.
Noh ehs too KOOL-pah, yoh loh see-EHN-toh

Please, give me another chance.
Por favor, dame otra oportunidad.
Pohr fah-VOHR, DAH-meh OH-trah oh-pohr-too-nee-DAHD

Will you ever forgive me?
¿Me perdonarás algún día?
Meh pehr-doh-nah-RAHS ahl-GOON DEE-ah

I hope in time we can still be friends.
Espero que con el tiempo podamos seguir siendo amigos.
Ehs-PEH-roh keh kohn ehl tee-EHM-poh poh-DAH-mohs seh-GEER see-EHN-doh ah-MEE-gohs

I screwed up, and I'm sorry.
Lo arruiné y lo lamento.
Loh ah-rroo-ee-NEH ee loh lah-MEHN-toh

SMALL TALK

No.
No.
Noh

Yes.
Sí.
See

Okay.
Ok.
Oh-KEH-ee

Please.
Por favor.
Pohr fah-VOHR

Do you fly out of the country often?
¿Vuelas fuera del país a menudo?
Voo-EH-lahs foo-EH-rah dehl pah-EES ah meh-NOO-doh

Thank you.
Gracias.
GRAH-see-ahs

That's okay.
Está bien.
Ehs-TAH bee-EHN

I went shopping.
Fui de compras.
Foo-EE deh KOHM-prahs

There.
Allí.
Ah-YEE

Very well.
Muy bien.
MOO-ee bee-EHN

What?
¿Qué?
Keh

I think you'll like it.
Creo que te gustará.
KREH-oh keh teh goos-tah-RAH

When?
¿Cuándo?
KWAHN-doh

I didn't sleep well.
No dormí bien.
Noh dohr-MEE bee-EHN

Until what time?
¿Hasta qué hora?
AHS-tah keh OH-rah

We are waiting in line.
Estamos esperando en la fila.
Ehs-TAH-mohs ehs-peh-RAHN-doh ehn lah FEE-lah

We're only waiting for a little bit longer.
Estamos esperando solo un poco más.
Ehs-TAH-mohs ehs-peh-RAHN-doh SOH-loh oon POH-koh mahs

How?
¿Cómo?
KOH-moh

Where?
¿Dónde?
DOHN-deh

I'm glad.
Me alegra.
Meh ah-LEH-grah

You are very tall.
Eres muy alto.
EH-rehs MOO-ee AHL-toh

I like to speak your language.
Me gusta hablar tu idioma.
Meh GOOS-tah ah-BLAHR too ee-dee-OH-mah

You are very kind.
Eres muy amable.
EH-rehs MOO-ee ah-MAH-bleh

Happy birthday!
¡Feliz cumpleaños!
Feh-LEES koom-pleh-AH-nyohs

I would like to thank you very much.
Quisiera agradecerte mucho.
Kee-see-EH-rah ah-grah-deh-SEHR-teh MOO-choh

Here is a gift that I bought for you.
Este es un regalo que compré para ti.
EHS-teh ehs oon rreh-GAH-loh keh kohm-PREH PAH-rah tee

Yes. Thank you for all of your help.
Sí. Gracias por toda tu ayuda.
See. GRAH-see-ahs pohr TOH-dah too ah-YOO-dah

What did you get?
¿Qué obtuviste?
Keh ohb-too-VEES-teh

Have a good trip!
¡Ten un buen viaje!
Tehn oon bwehn vee-AH-heh

This place is very special to me.
Este lugar es muy especial para mí.
EHS-teh loo-GAHR ehs MOO-ee ehs-peh-see-AHL PAH-rah mee

My foot is asleep.
Mi pie está dormido.
Mee pee-EH ehs-TAH dohr-MEE-doh

May I open this now or later?
¿Puedo abrir esto ya o después?
PWEH-doh ah-BREER EHS-toh yah oh dehs-PWEHS

Why do you think that is?
¿Por qué crees que sea?
Pohr keh KREH-ehs keh SEH-ah

Which do you like better, chocolate or caramel?
¿Qué te gusta más: el chocolate o el caramelo?
Keh teh GOOS-tah mahs, ehl choh-koh-LAH-teh oh ehl kah-rah-MEH-loh

Be safe on your journey.
Ve seguro en tu viaje.
Veh seh-GOO-roh ehn too vee-AH-heh

I want to do this for a little longer.
Quiero hacer esto por un poco más de tiempo.
Kee-EH-roh ah-SEHR EHS-toh pohr oon POH-koh mahs deh tee-EHM-poh

This is a picture that I took at the hotel.
Esta es una foto que tomé en el hotel.
EHS-tah ehs OO-nah FOH-toh keh toh-MEH ehn ehl oh-TEHL

Allow me.
Permíteme.
Pehr-MEE-teh-meh

I was surprised.
Estaba sorprendida.
Ehs-TAH-bah sohr-prehn-DEE-dah

I like that.
Me gusta eso.
Meh GOOS-tah EH-soh

Are you in high spirits today?
¿Estás de buen humor hoy?
Ehs-TAHS deh bwehn oo-MOHR OH-ee

Oh, here comes my wife.
Oh, ahí viene mi esposa.
Oh, ah-EE vee-EH-neh mee ehs-POH-sah

Can I see the photograph?
¿Puedo ver la fotografía?
PWEH-doh vehr lah foh-toh-grah-FEE-ah

Feel free to ask me anything.
Siéntete libre de preguntarme cualquier cosa.
See-EHN-teh-teh LEE-breh deh preh-goon-TAHR-meh koo-ahl-kee-EHR
KOH-sah

That was magnificent!
¡Eso estuvo magnífico!
EH-soh ehs-TOO-voh mahg-NEE-fee-koh

See you some other time.
Te veo en otra ocasión.
Teh VEH-oh ehn OH-trah oh-kah-see-OHN

No more, please.
No más, por favor.
Noh mahs, pohr fah-VOHR

Please don't use that.
Por favor, no uses eso.
Pohr fah-VOHR, noh OO-sehs EH-soh

That is very pretty.
Eso está muy bonito.
EH-soh ehs-TAH MOO-ee boh-NEE-toh

Would you say that again?
¿Dirías eso otra otra vez?
Dee-REE-ahs EH-soh OH-trah vehs

Speak slowly.
Habla despacio.
AH-blah dehs-PAH-see-oh

I'm home.
Estoy en casa.
Ehs-TOH-ee ehn KAH-sah

Is this your home?
¿Esta es tu casa?
EHS-tah ehs too KAH-sah

I know a lot about the area.
Sé mucho sobre el área.
Seh MOO-choh SOH-breh ehl AH-reh-ah

Welcome back. How was your day?
Bienvenido otra vez. ¿Cómo estuvo tu día?
Bee-ehn-veh-NEE-doh OH-trah vehs. KOH-moh ehs-TOO-voh too DEE-ah

I read every day.
Yo leo todos los días.
Yoh LEH-oh TOH-dohs lohs DEE-ahs

My favorite type of book are novels by Stephen King.
Mi tipo de libro favorito son las novelas de Stephen King.
Mee TEE-poh deh LEE-broh fah-voh-REE-toh sohn lahs noh-VEH-lahs deh
Stephen King.

You surprised me!
¡Me sorprendieron!
Meh sohr-prehn-dee-EH-rohn

I am short on time, so I have to go.
Estoy corto de tiempo, así que me tengo que ir.
Ehs-TOH-ee KOHR-toh deh tee-EHM-poh, ah-SEE keh meh TEHN-goh keh
eer

Thank you for having this conversation.
Gracias por tener esta conversación.
GRAH-see-ahs pohr teh-NEHR EHS-tah kohn-vehr-sah-see-OHN

Oh, when is it?
Oh, ¿cuándo es eso?
Oh, KWAHN-doh ehs EH-soh

This is my brother Jeremy.
Este es mi hermano, Jeremy.
EHS-teh ehs mee ehr-MAH-noh, YEH-reh-mee

That is my favorite bookstore.
Esa es mi librería favorita.
EH-sah ehs mee lee-breh-REE-ah fah-voh-REE-tah

That statue is bigger than it looks.
La estatua es más grande de lo que parece.
Lah ehs-TAH-too-ah ehs mahs GRAHN-deh deh loh keh pah-REH-seh

Look at the shape of that cloud!
¡Mira la forma de esa nube!
MEE-rah lah FOHR-mah deh EH-sah NOO-beh

BUSINESS

I am president of the credit union.
Soy el presidente de la unión de crédito.
SOH-ee ehl preh-see-DEHN-teh deh lah oo-nee-OHN deh KREH-dee-toh

We are expanding in your area.
Estamos expandiéndonos en tu área.
Ehs-TAH-mohs ehks-pahn-dee-EHN-doh-nohs ehn too AH-reh-ah

I am looking for work in the agriculture field.
Estoy buscando trabajo en el campo de la agricultura.
Ehs-TOH-ee boos-KAHN-doh trah-BAH-hoh ehn ehl KAHM-poh deh lah
ah-gree-kool-TOO-rah

Sign here, please.
Firme aquí, por favor.
FEER-meh ah-KEE, pohr fah-VOHR

I am looking for temporary work.
Estoy buscando un trabajo temporal.
Ehs-TOH-ee boos-KAHN-doh oon trah-BAH-hoh tehm-poh-RAHL

I need to call and set up that meeting.
Necesito llamar y programar esa reunión.
Neh-seh-SEE-toh yah-MAHR ee proh-grah-MAHR EH-sah rreh-oo-nee-
OHN

Is the line open?
¿La línea está abierta?
Lah LEE-neh-ah ehs-TAH ah-bee-EHR-tah

I need you to hang up the phone.
Necesito que cuelgues el teléfono.
Neh-seh-SEE-toh keh koo-EHL-gehs ehl teh-LEH-foh-noh

Who should I ask for more information about your business?
¿A quién debería pedirle más información sobre tu negocio?
Ah kee-EHN deh-beh-REE-ah peh-DEER-leh mahs een-fohr-mah-see-OHN SOH-breh too neh-GOH-see-oh

There was no answer when you handed me the phone.
No hubo respuesta cuando me pasaste el teléfono.
Noh OO-boh rrehs-PWEHS-tah KWAHN-doh meh pah-SAHS-teh ehl teh-LEH-foh-noh

Robert is not here at the moment.
Robert no está aquí por el momento.
Robert noh ehs-TAH ah-KEE pohr ehl moh-MEHN-toh

Call me after work, thanks.
Llámame después del trabajo, gracias.
YAH-mah-meh dehs-PWEHS dehl trah-BAH-hoh, GRAH-see-ahs

We're strongly considering your contract offer.
Estamos considerando seriamente tu oferta de contrato.
Ehs-TAH-mohs kohn-see-deh-RAHN-doh seh-ree-ah-MEHN-teh too oh-FEHR-tah deh kohn-TRAH-toh

Have the necessary forms been signed yet?
¿Ya se han firmado los formularios necesarios?
Yah seh ahn feer-MAH-doh lohs fohr-moo-LAH-ree-ohs neh-seh-SAH-ree-ohs

I have a few hours available after work.
Tengo unas horas disponibles después del trabajo.
TEHN-goh OO-nahs OH-rahs dees-poh-NEE-blehs dehs-PWEHS dehl trah-BAH-hoh

What do they make there?
¿Qué hacen ellos allí?
Keh AH-sehn EH-yohs ah-YEE

I have no tasks assigned to me.
No tengo tareas asignadas para mí.
Noh TEHN-goh tah-REH-ahs ah-seeg-NAH-dahs PAH-rah mee

How many workers are they hiring?
¿Cuántos trabajadores están contratando?
KWAHN-tohs trah-bah-hah-DOH-rehs ehs-TAHN kohn-trah-TAHN-doh

It should take me three hours to complete this task.
Debería tomarme unas tres horas completar esta tarea.
Deh-beh-REE-ah toh-MAHR-meh OO-nahs trehs OH-rahs kohm-pleh-TAHR EHS-tah tah-REH-ah

Don't use that computer, it is only for financial work.
No uses ese computador, es solo para el trabajo financiero.

Noh OO-sehs EH-seh kohm-poo-tah-DOHR, ehs SOH-loh PAH-rah ehl trah-BAH-hoh fee-nahn-see-EH-roh

I only employ people that I can rely on.
Yo solo empleo a personas en las que puedo confiar.
Yoh SOH-loh ehm-PLEH-oh ah pehr-SOHN-nahs ehn lahs keh PWEH-doh kohn-fee-AHR

After I talk to my lawyers, we can discuss this further.
Podemos seguir discutiendo esto después de que hable con mis abogados.
Poh-DEH-mohs see-GEER dees-koo-tee-EHN-doh EHS-toh dehs-PWEHS deh keh AH-bleh kohn mees ah-boh-GAH-dohs

Are there any open positions in my field?
¿Hay alguna posición disponible en mi campo?
AH-ee ahl-GOO-nah poh-see-see-OHN dees-poh-NEE-bleh ehn mee KAHM-poh

I'll meet you in the conference room.
Te veré en la sala de conferencias.
Teh veh-REH ehn lah SAH-lah deh kohn-feh-REHN-see-ahs

Call and leave a message on my office phone.
Llama al número de mi oficina y deja un mensaje.
YAH-mah ahl NOO-meh-roh deh mee oh-fee-SEE-nah ee DEH-hah oon mehn-SAH-heh

Send me a fax with that information.
Envíame un fax con esa información.
Ehn-VEE-ah-meh oon fahks kohn EH-sah een-fohr-mah-see-OHN

Hi, I would like to leave a message for Sheila.
Hola, quisiera dejar un mensaje para Sheila.
OH-lah, kee-see-EH-rah deh-HAHR oon mehn-SAH-heh PAH-rah Sheila

Please repeat your last name.
Por favor, repite tu apellido.
Pohr fah-VOHR, rreh-PEE-teh too ah-peh-YEE-doh

I would like to buy wholesale.
Me gustaría comprar al por mayor.
Meh goos-tah-REE-ah kohm-PRAHR ahl pohr mah-YOHR

How do you spell your last name?
¿Cómo deletreas tu apellido?
KOH-moh deh-leh-TREH-ahs too ah-peh-YEE-doh

I called your boss yesterday and left a message.
Llamé a tu jefe ayer y dejé un mensaje.
Yah-MEH ah too HEH-feh ah-YEHR ee deh-HEH oon mehn-SAH-heh

That customer hung up on me.
Ese cliente me colgó.
EH-seh klee-EHN-teh meh kohl-GOH

She called but didn't leave a callback number.
Ella llamó, pero no dejó un número para devolverle la llamada.
EH-yah yah-MOH, PEH-roh noh deh-HOH oon NOO-meh-roh PAH-rah
deh-vohl-VEHR-leh lah yah-MAH-da

Hello! Am I speaking to Bob?
¡Hola! ¿Estoy hablando con Bob?
OH-lah. Ehs-TOH-ee ah-BLAHN-doh kohn Bob

Excuse me, but could you speak up? I can't hear you.
Disculpe, pero ¿puede hablar más alto? No puedo escucharlo.
Dees-KOOL-peh, PEH-roh PWEH-deh ah-BLAHR mahs AHL-toh. Noh
PWEH-doh ehs-koo-CHAHR-loh

The line is very bad, could you move to a different area so I can hear you better?
La señal es muy mala, ¿podrías moverte a un área diferente para que yo
pueda escucharte mejor?
Lah seh-NYAHL ehs MOO-ee MAH-lah, poh-DREE-ahs moh-VEHR-teh ah
oon AH-reh-ah dee-feh-REHN-teh PAH-rah keh yoh PWEH-dah ehs-koo-
CHAHR-teh meh-HOHR

I would like to apply for a work visa.
Quisiera aplicar para una visa de trabajo.
Kee-see-EH-rah ah-plee-KAHR PAH-rah OO-nah VEE-sah deh trah-BAH-hoh

It is my dream to work here teaching the language.
Mi sueño es trabajar aquí enseñando el idioma.
Mee soo-EH-nyoh ehs trah-bah-HAHR ah-KEE ehn-seh-NYAHN-doh ehl ee-dee-OH-mah

I have always wanted to work here.
Siempre he querido trabajar aquí.
See-EHM-preh eh keh-REE-doh trah-bah-HAHR ah-KEE

Where do you work?
¿Dónde trabajas?
DOHN-deh trah-BAH-hahs

Are we in the same field of work?
¿Estamos en el mismo campo de trabajo?
Ehs-TAH-mohs ehn ehl MEES-moh KAHM-poh deh trah-BAH-hoh

Do we share an office?
¿Compartimos una oficina?
Kohm-pahr-TEE-mohs OO-nah oh-fee-SEE-nah

What do you do for a living?
¿En qué trabajas?
Ehn keh trah-BAH-hahs

I work in the city as an engineer for Cosco.
Trabajo en la ciudad, como ingeniero, para Cosco.
Trah-BAH-hoh ehn lah see-oo-DAHD, KOH-moh een-heh-nee-EH-roh, PAH-rah Cosco

I am an elementary teacher.
Soy profesor de primaria.
SOH-ee proh-feh-SOHR deh pree-MAH-ree-ah

What time should I be at the meeting?
¿A qué hora debería estar en la reunión?
Ah keh OH-rah deh-beh-REE-ah ehs-TAHR ehn lah rreh-oo-nee-OHN

Would you like me to catch you up on what the meeting was about?
¿Quisieras que te ponga al día sobre qué se trató la reunión?
Kee-see-EH-rahs keh teh POHN-gah ahl DEE-ah SOH-breh keh seh trah-TOH lah rreh-oo-nee-OHN

I would like to set up a meeting with your company.
Quisiera agendar una reunión con su compañía.
Kee-see-EH-rah ah-hehn-DAHR OO-nah rreh-oo-nee-OHN kohn soo kohm-pah-NYEE-ah

Please, call my secretary for that information.
Por favor, llama a mi secretaria para esa información.
Pohr fah-VOHR, YAH-mah ah mee seh-kreh-TAH-ree-ah PAH-rah EH-sah een-fohr-mah-see-OHN

I will have to ask my lawyer.
Tendré que preguntarle a mi abogado.
Tehn-DREH keh preh-goon-TAHR-leh ah mee ah-boh-GAH-doh

Fax it over to my office number.
Envíalo por fax al número de mi oficina.
Ehn-VEE-ah-loh pohr fahks ahl NOO-meh-roh deh mee oh-fee-SEE-nah

Will I have any trouble calling into the office?
¿Tendré algún problema llamando a la oficina?
Tehn-DREH ahl-GOON proh-BLEH-mah yah-MAHN-doh ah lah oh-fee-SEE-nah

Do you have a business card I can have?
¿Tienes una tarjeta comercial que yo pueda tener?
Tee-EH-nehs OO-nah tahr-HEH-tah koh-mehr-see-AHL keh yoh PWEH-dah teh-NEHR

Here is my business card. Please, take it.
Aquí está mi tarjeta comercial. Por favor, tómala.
Ah-KEE ehs-TAH mee tahr-HEH-tah koh-mehr-see-AHL. Pohr fah-VOHR, TOH-mah-lah

My colleague and I are going to lunch.
Mi colega y yo vamos a almorzar.
Mee koh-LEH-gah ee yoh VAH-mohs ah ahl-mohr-SAHR

I am the director of finance for my company.
Soy el director de Finanzas de mi compañía
SOH-ee ehl dee-rehk-TOHR deh fee-NAHN-sahs deh mee kohm-pah-NYEE-ah

I manage the import goods of my company.
Yo gestiono las mercancías de importación de mi compañía.
Yoh hehs-tee-OH-noh lahs mehr-kahn-SEE-ahs deh eem-pohr-tah-see-OHN deh mee kohm-pah-NYEE-ah

My colleagues' boss is Steven.
El jefe de mis colegas es Steven.
Ehl HEH-feh deh mees koh-LEH-gahs ehs Steven

I work for the gas station company.
Yo trabajo para la compañía de la estación de gasolina.
Yoh trah-BAH-hoh PAH-rah lah kohm-pah-NYEE-ah deh lah ehs-tah-see-OHN deh gah-soh-LEE-nah

What company do you work for?
¿Para qué compañía trabajas?
PAH-rah keh kohm-pah-NYEE-ah trah-BAH-hahs

I'm an independent contractor.
Soy un contratista independiente.
SOH-ee oon kohn-trah-TEES-tah een-deh-pehn-dee-EHN-teh

How many employees do you have at your company?
¿Cuántos empleados tienen en tu compañía?
KWAHN-tohs ehm-pleh-AH-dohs tee-EH-nehn ehn too kohm-pah-NYEE-ah

I know a lot about engineering.
Sé mucho sobre ingeniería.
Seh MOO-choh SOH-breh een-heh-nee-eh-REE-ah

I can definitely resolve that dispute for you.
Yo puedo resolver definitivamente esa disputa por usted.

Yoh PWEH-doh rreh-sohl-VEHR deh-fee-nee-tee-vah-MEHN-teh EH-sah dees-POO-tah pohr oos-TEHD

You should hire an interpreter.
Deberías contratar a un intérprete.
Deh-beh-REE-ahs kohn-trah-TAHR ah oon een-TEHR-preh-teh

Are you hiring any additional workers?
¿Están contratando algunos trabajadores adicionales?
Ehs-TAHN kohn-trah-TAHN-doh ahl-GOO-nohs trah-bah-hah-DOH-rehs
ah-dee-see-oh-NAH-lehs

How much experience do I need to work here?
¿Cuánta experiencia necesito para trabajar aquí?
KWAHN-tah ehks-peh-ree-EHN-see-ah neh-seh-SEE-toh PAH-rah trah-
bah-HAHR ah-KEE

Our marketing manager handles that.
Nuestro gerente de mercadeo maneja eso.
NWEHS-troh heh-REHN-teh deh mehr-kah-DEH-oh mah-NEH-hah EH-soh

I would like to poach one of your workers.
Me gustaría llevarme a uno de tus trabajadores.
Meh goos-tah-REE-ah yeh-VAHR-meh ah OO-noh deh toos trah-bah-
hah-DOH-rehs

Can we work out a deal that is beneficial for the both of us?
¿Podemos llegar a un acuerdo que sea beneficioso para los dos?
Poh-DEH-mohs yeh-GAHR ah oon ah-koo-EHR-doh keh SEH-ah beh-neh-
fee-see-OH-soh PAH-rah lohs dohs

My resources are at your disposal.
Mis recursos están a tu disposición.
Mees rreh-KOOR-sohs ehs-TAHN ah too dees-poh-see-see-OHN

I am afraid that we have to let you go.
Me temo que tenemos que dejarte ir.
Meh TEH-moh keh teh-NEH-mohs keh deh-HAHR-teh eer

This is your first warning. Please don't do that again.
Esta es tu primera advertencia. Por favor, no lo vuelvas a hacer.
EHS-tah ehs too pree-MEH-rah ahd-vehr-TEHN-see-ah. Pohr fah-VOHR,
noh loh voo-EHL-vahs ah ah-SEHR

File a complaint with HR about the incident.
Presenta una queja a recursos humanos sobre el incidente.
Preh-SEHN-tah OO-nah KEH-hah ah rreh-KOOR-sohs oo-MAH-nohs SOH-
breh ehl een-see-DEHN-teh

Who is showing up for our lunch meeting?
¿Quién va a presentarse en nuestra reunión de almuerzo?
Kee-EHN vah ah preh-sehn-TAHR-seh ehn NWEHS-trah rreh-oo-nee-OHN deh ahl-moo-EHR-soh

Clear out the rest of my day.
Libera el resto de mi día.
Lee-BEH-rah ehl RREHS-toh deh mee DEE-ah

We need to deposit this into the bank.
Necesitamos depositar esto en el banco.
Neh-seh-see-TAH-mohs deh-poh-see-TAHR EHS-toh ehn ehl BAHN-koh

Can you cover the next hour for me?
¿Puedes cubrir la siguiente hora por mí?
PWEH-dehs koo-BREER lah see-gee-EHN-teh OH-rah pohr mee

If Shania calls, please push her directly through.
Si Shania llama, me la pasas directamente, por favor.
See Shania YAH-mah, meh lah PAH-sahs dee-rehk-tah-MEHN-teh, pohr fah-VOHR

I'm leaving early today.
Hoy me estoy yendo temprano.
OH-ee meh ehs-TOH-ee YEHN-doh tehm-PRAH-noh

I'll be working late tonight.
Esta noche estaré trabajando hasta tarde.
EHS-tah NOH-cheh ehs-tah-REH trah-bah-HAHN-doh AHS-tah TAHR-deh

You can use the bathroom in my office.
Puedes usar el baño en mi oficina.
PWEH-dehs oo-SAHR ehl BAH-nyoh ehn mee oh-fee-SEE-nah

You can use my office phone to call out.
Puedes usar el teléfono de mi oficina para llamar.
PWEH-dehs oo-SAHR ehl teh-LEH-foh-noh deh mee oh-fee-SEE-nah PAH-rah yah-MAHR

Please, close the door behind you.
Por favor, cierra la puerta detrás de ti.
Pohr fah-VOHR, see-EH-rrah lah PWEHR-tah deh-TRAHS deh tee

I need to talk to you privately.
Necesito hablarte en privado.
Neh-seh-SEE-toh ah-BLAHR-teh ehn pree-VAH-doh

Your team is doing good work on this project.
Tu equipo está haciendo un buen trabajo en este proyecto.
Too eh-KEE-poh ehs-TAH ah-see-EHN-doh oon bwehn trah-BAH-hoh ehn
EHS-teh proh-YEHK-toh

Our numbers are down this quarter.
Nuestros números son bajos este trimestre.
NWEHS-trohs NOO-meh-rohs sohn BAH-hohs EHS-teh tree-MEHS-treh

I need you to work harder than usual.
Necesito que trabajes más duro de lo normal.
Neh-seh-SEE-toh keh trah-BAH-hehs mahs DOO-roh deh loh norh-MAHL

I'm calling in sick today. Can anyone cover my shift?
Estoy reportándome enfermo hoy. ¿Alguien puede cubrir mi turno?
Ehs-TOH-ee rreh-pohr-TAHN-doh-meh ehn-FEHR-moh OH-ee. AHL-gee-
ehn PWEH-deh koo-BREER mee TOOR-noh

Tom, we are thinking of promoting you.
Tom, estamos pensando en promoverte.
Tom, ehs-TAH-mohs pehn-SAHN-doh ehn proh-moh-VEHR-teh

I would like a raise.
Quisiera un aumento.
Kee-see-EH-rah oon ah-oo-MEHN-toh

THE WEATHER

I think the weather is changing.
Creo que el clima está cambiando.
KRE-oh keh ehl KLEE-mah ehs-TAH kahm-bee-AHN-doh

Be careful, it is raining outside.
Ten cuidado, está lloviendo afuera.
Tehn koo-ee-DAH-doh, ehs-TAH yoh-vee-EHN-doh ah-foo-EH-rah

Make sure to bring your umbrella
Asegúrate de traer tu paraguas.
Ah-seh-GOO-rah-teh deh trah-EHR too pah-RAH-goo-ahs

Get out of the rain or you will catch a cold.
Sal de la lluvia o vas a coger un resfriado.
Sahl deh lah YOO-vee-ah oh vahs ah koh-HEHR oon rrehs-free-AH-doh

Is it snowing?
¿Está nevando?
Ehs-TAH neh-VAHN-doh

The snow is very thick right now.
La nieve está muy gruesa ahora mismo.
Lah nee-EH-veh ehs-TAH MOO-ee groo-EH-sah ah-OH-rah MEES-moh

Be careful, the road is full of ice.
Ten cuidado, el camino está lleno de hielo.
Tehn koo-ee-DAH-doh, ehl kah-MEE-noh ehs-TAH YEH-noh deh ee-EH-loh

What is the climate like here? Is it warm or cold?
¿Cómo es el clima aquí? ¿Es cálido o frío?
KOH-moh ehs ehl KLEE-mah ah-KEE. Ehs KAH-lee-doh oh FREE-oh

It has been a very nice temperature here.
Ha habido una temperatura muy agradable aquí.
Ah ah-BEE-doh OO-nah tehm-peh-rah-TOO-rah MOO-ee ah-grah-DAH-bleh ah-KEE

Does it rain a lot here?
¿Llueve mucho aquí?
Yoo-EH-veh MOO-choh ah-KEE

The temperature is going to break records this week.
La temperatura va a romper récords esta semana
Lah tehm-peh-rah-TOO-rah vah ah rrohm-PEHR RREH-kohrds EHS-tah
seh-MAH-nah

Does it ever snow here?
Nieva alguna vez aquí.
Nee-EH-vah ahl-GOO-nah vehs ah-KEE

When does it get sunny?
¿Cuándo se pone soleado?
KWAHN-doh seh POH-neh soh-leh-AH-doh

What's the forecast look like for tomorrow?
¿Cuál es el pronóstico del clima para mañana?
Kwahl ehs ehl proh-NOHS-tee-koh dehl KLEE-mah PAH-rah mah-NYAH-
nah

This is a heatwave.
Esta es una ola de calor.
EHS-tah ehs OO-nah OH-lah deh kah-LOHR

Right now it is overcast, but should clear up by this evening.
Ahora mismo está nublado, pero en la tarde debería aclararse.
Ah-OH-rah MEES-moh ehs-TAH noo-BLAH-doh, PEH-roh ehn lah TAHR-
deh deh-beh-REE-ah ah-klah-RAHR-seh

It is going to heat up in the afternoon.
En la tarde se calentará el clima.
Ehn lah TAHR-deh seh kah-lehn-tah-RAH ehl KLEE-mah

What channel is the weather channel?
¿Cuál es el canal del clima?
Kwahl ehs ehl kah-NAHL dehl KLEE-mah

Tonight it will be below freezing.
Esta noche la temperatura estará bajo cero.
EHS-tah NOH-cheh lah tehm-peh-rah-TOO-rah ehs-tah-RAH BAH-hoh
SEH-roh

It's very windy outside.
Hace mucho viento afuera.
AH-seh MOO-choh vee-EHN-toh ah-foo-EH-rah

It's going to be cold in the morning.
Hará frío en la mañana.
Ah-RAH FREE-oh ehn lah mah-NYAH-nah

It's not raining, only drizzling.
No está lloviendo, solo lloviznando.
Noh ehs-TAH yoh-vee-EHN-doh, SOH-loh yoh-vees-NAHN-doh

HOTEL

I would like to book a room.
Me gustaría reservar una habitación.
Meh goos-tah-REE-ah rreh-sehr-VAHR OO-nah ah-bee-tah-see-OHN

I'd like a single room.
Quisiera una habitación individual.
Kee-see-EH-rah OO-nah ah-bee-tah-see-OHN eehn-dee-vee-DOOAHL

I'd like a suite.
Quisiera una suite.
Kee-see-EH-rah OO-nah suite.

How much is the room per night?
¿Cuánto cuesta la habitación por noche?
KWAHN-toh KWEHS-tah lah ah-bee-tah-see-OHN pohr NOH-cheh

How much is the room with tax?
¿Cuánto cuesta la habitación con impuestos incluidos?
KWAHN-toh KWEHS-tah lah ah-bee-tah-see-OHN kohn eem-PWEHS-tohs een-kloo-EE-dohs

When is the checkout time?
¿Cuándo es la hora de salida?
KWAHN-doh ehs lah OH-rah deh sah-LEE-dah

I'd like a room with a nice view.
Quisiera una habitación con una bonita vista.
Kee-see-EH-rah OO-nah ah-bee-tah-see-OHN kohn OO-nah boh-NEE-tah VEES-tah

I'd like to order room service.
Quisiera ordenar servicio a la habitación.
Kee-see-EH-rah ohr-deh-NAHR sehr-VEE-see-oh ah lah ah-bee-tah-see-OHN

Let's go swim in the outdoor pool.
Vamos a nadar en la piscina exterior.
VAH-mohs ah nah-DAHR ehn lah pee-SEE-nah ehks-teh-ree-OHR

Are pets allowed at the hotel?
¿Las mascotas están permitidas en el hotel?
Lahs mahs-KOH-tahs ehs-TAHN pehr-mee-TEE-dahs ehn ehl oh-TEHL

I would like a room on the first floor.
Quisiera una habitación en el primer piso.
Kee-see-EH-rah OO-nah ah-bee-tah-see-OHN.ehn ehl pree-MEHR PEE-soh

Can you send maintenance up to our room for a repair?
¿Pueden enviar al equipo de mantenimiento arriba, a nuestra habitación, para una reparación?
PWEH-dehn ehn-vee-AHR ahl eh-KEE-poh deh mahn-teh-nee-mee-EHN-toh ah-RREE-bah, ah NWEHS-trah ah-bee-tah-see-OHN, PAH-rah OO-nah rreh-pah-rah-see-OHN

I'm locked out of my room, could you unlock it?
Estoy bloqueado fuera de mi habitación, ¿podrías desbloquear el acceso?
Ehs-TOH-ee bloh-keh-AH-doh foo-EH-rah deh mee ah-bee-tah-see-OHN, poh-DREE-ahs dehs-bloh-keh-AHR ehl ahk-SEH-soh

Our door is jammed and won't open.
Nuestra puerta está trabada y no se abrirá.
NWEHS-trah poo-ERH-tah ehs-TAH trah-BAH-dah ee noh seh ah-bree-RAH

How do you work the shower?
¿Cómo haces funcionar la ducha?
KOH-moh AH-sehs foon-see-oh-NAHR lah DOO-chah

Are the consumables in the room free?
¿Los consumibles en la habitación son gratis?
Lohs kohn-soo-MEE-blehs ehn lah ah-bee-tah-see-OHN sohn GRAH-tees

What is my final bill for the stay, including incidentals?
¿Cuánto es la cuenta final por mi estadía, con gastos incidentales incluidos?
KWAHN-toh ehs lah KWEHN-tah fee-NAHL pohr mee ehs-tah-DEE-ah, kohn GAHS-tohs een-cee-dehn-TAH-lehs een-kloo-EE-dohs

Can you show me my room?
¿Puedes mostrarme mi habitación?
PWEH-dehs mohs-TRAHR-meh mee ah-bee-tah-see-OHN

Where can I get ice for my room?
¿Dónde puedo conseguir hielo para mi habitación?
DOHN-deh PWEH-doh kohn-seh-GEER ee-EH-loh PAH-rah mee ah-bee-tah-see-OHN

Do you have any rooms available?
¿Tienen algunas habitaciones disponibles?
Tee-EH-nehn ahl-GOO-nahs ah-bee-tah-see-OHN-nehs dees-poh-NEE-blehs

Do you sell bottled water?
¿Venden agua embotellada?
VEHN-dehn AH-goo-ah ehm-boh-teh-YAH-dah

Our towels are dirty.
Nuestras toallas están sucias.
NWEHS-trahs toh-AH-yahs ehs-TAHN SOO-see-ahs

Have you stayed at this hotel before?
¿Te has quedado en este hotel antes?
Teh ahs keh-DAH-doh ehn EHS-teh oh-TEHL AHN-tehs

How much is a room for two adults?
¿Cuánto cuesta una habitación para dos adultos?
KWAHN-toh KWEHS-tah OO-nah ah-bee-tah-see-OHN PAH-rah dohs ah-DOOL-tohs

Does the room come with a microwave?
¿La habitación viene con un microondas?
Lah ah-bee-tah-see-OHN vee-EH-neh kohn oon mee-kroh-OHN-dahs

May I see the room first? That way I will know if I like it.
¿Puedo ver la habitación primero? De esa manera sabré si me gusta.
PWEH-doh vehr lah ah-bee-tah-see-OHN pree-MEH-roh deh EH-sah mah-NEH-rah sah-BREH see meh GOOS-tah

Do you have a room that is quieter?
¿Tienes una habitación que sea más silenciosa?
Tee-EH-nehs OO-nah ah-bee-tah-see-OHN keh SEH-ah mahs see-lehn-see-OH-sah

How much is the deposit for my stay?
¿Cuánto es el depósito por mi estadía?
KWAHN-toh ehs ehl deh-POH-see-toh pohr mee ehs-tah-DEE-ah

Is the tap water drinkable at the hotel?
¿El agua del grifo es potable en el hotel?
Ehl AH-goo-ah dehl GREE-foh ehs poh-TAH-bleh ehn ehl oh-TEHL

Will there be any holds on my credit card?
¿Habrá alguna retención en mi tarjeta de crédito?
Ah-BRAH ahl-GOO-nah rreh-tehn-see-OHN ehn mee tahr-HEH-tah deh KREH-dee-toh

Can I get a replacement room key?
¿Pueden darme una llave de reemplazo para mi habitación?
PWEH-dehn DAHR-meh OO-nah YAH-veh deh rreh-ehm-PLAH-soh PAH-rah mee ah-bee-tah-see-OHN

How much is a replacement room key?
¿Cuánto cuesta una llave de reemplazo para la habitación?
KWAHN-toh KWEHS-tah OO-nah YAH-veh deh rreh-ehm-PLAH-soh PAH-rah lah ah-bee-tah-see-OHN

Does the bathroom have a shower or a bathtub?
¿El baño tiene una ducha o una tina?
Ehl BAH-nyoh tee-EH-neh OO-nah DOO-chah oh OO-nah TEE-nah

Are any of the channels on the tv available in English?
¿Hay alguno de los canales en la televisión disponible en inglés?
AH-ee ahl-GOO-noh deh lohs kah-NAH-lehs ehn lah teh-leh-vee-see-OHN dees-poh-NEE-bleh ehn een-GLEHS

I want a bigger room.
Quiero una habitación más grande.
Kee-EH-roh OO-nah ah-bee-tah-see-OHN mahs GRAHN-deh

Do you serve breakfast in the morning?
¿Sirven desayuno en la mañana?
SEER-vehn deh-sah-YOO-noh ehn lah mah-NYAH-nah

Oh, it's spacious.
Oh, es espacioso.
Oh, ehs ehs-pah-see-OH-soh

My room is this way.
Mi habitación está por aquí.
Mee ah-bee-tah-see-OHN ehs-TAH pohr ah-KEE

Straight down the hall.
Recto por el corredor.
RREHK-toh pohr ehl koh-rreh-DOHR

Can you suggest a different hotel?
¿Puedes sugerirme otro hotel?
PWEH-dehs soo-heh-REER-meh OH-troh oh-TEHL

Does the room have a safe for my valuables?
¿La habitación tiene una caja fuerte para mis objetos de valor?
Lah ah-bee-tah-see-OHN tee-EH-neh OO-nah KAH-hah foo-EHR-teh PAH-rah mees ohb-HEH-tohs deh vah-LOHR

Please clean my room.
Por favor, limpie mi habitación.
Pohr fah-VOHR, LEEM-pee-eh mee ah-bee-tah-see-OHN

Don't disturb me, please.
Por favor, no me moleste.
Pohr fah-VOHR, noh meh moh-LEHS-teh

Can you wake me up at noon?
¿Puedes despertarme a mediodía?
PWEH-dehs dehs-pehr-TAHR-meh ah meh-dee-oh-DEE-ah

I would like to check out of my hotel room.
Quisiera registrar la salida de mi habitación de hotel.
Kee-see-EH-rah rreh-hees-TRAHR lah sah-LEE-dah deh mee ah-bee-tah-see-OHN deh oh-TEHL

Please increase the cleanup duty of my hotel room.
Por favor, aumenta la labor de limpieza de mi habitación de hotel.
Pohr fah-VOHR, ah-oo-MEHN-tah lah lah-BOHR deh leem-pee-EH-sah deh mee ah-bee-tah-see-OHN deh oh-TEHL

Is the Marriott any good?
¿El Marriott es bueno?
Ehl Marriott ehs BWEH-noh

Is it expensive to stay at the Marriott?
¿Es costoso hospedarse en el Marriott?
Ehs kohs-TOH-soh ohs-peh-DAHR-seh ehn ehl Marriott

I think our room has bed bugs.
Creo que nuestra habitación tiene chinches.
KREH-oh keh NWEHS-trah ah-bee-tah-see-OHN tee-EH-neh CHEEN-chehs

Can you send an exterminator to our room?
¿Pueden enviar un exterminador a nuestra habitación?
PWEH-dehn ehn-vee-AHR oon ehks-tehr-mee-nah-DOHR ah NWEHS-trah ah-bee-tah-see-OHN

I need to speak to your manager.
Necesito hablar con su gerente.
Neh-seh-SEE-toh ah-BLAHR kohn soo heh-REHN-teh

Do you have the number to corporate?
¿Tienes el número del corporativo?
Tee-EH-nehs oon NOO-meh-roh dehl kohr-poh-rah-TEE-voh

Does the hotel shuttle go to the casino?
¿El transporte del hotel va al casino?
Ehl trahns-POHR-teh dehl oh-TEHL vah ahl kah-SEE-noh

Can you call me when the hotel shuttle is on its way?
¿Puedes llamarme cuando el transporte del hotel esté en camino?
PWEH-dehs yah-MAHR-meh KWAHN-doh ehl trahns-POHR-teh dehl oh-TEHL ehs-TEH ehn kah-MEE-noh

Can we reserve this space for a party?
¿Podemos reservar este espacio para una fiesta?
Poh-DEH-mohs rreh-sehr-VAHR EHS-teh ehs-PAH-see-oh PAH-rah OO-nah fee-EHS-tah

What is the guest limit for reserving an area?
¿Cuál es el límite de invitados para reservar esta área?
Kwahl ehs ehl LEE-mee-teh deh een-vee-TAH-dohs PAH-rah rreh-sehr-VAHR EHS-tah AH-reh-ah

What are the rules for reserving an area?
¿Cuáles son las reglas para reservar un área?
KWAH-lehs sohn lahs RREH-glahs PAH-rah rreh-sehr-VAHR oon AH-reh-ah

Can we serve or drink alcohol during our get together?
¿Podemos servir o tomar alcohol durante nuestra fiesta?
Poh-DEH-mohs sehr-VEER oh toh-MAHR ahl-koh-OHL doo-RAHN-teh NWEHS-trah fee-EHS-tah

I would like to complain about a noisy room next to us.
Quisiera quejarme sobre una habitación ruidosa cercana a la nuestra.
Kee-see-EH-rah keh-HAHR-meh SOH-breh OO-nah ah-bee-tah-see-OHN rroo-ee-DOH-sah sehr-KAH-nah ah lah NWEHS-trah

We have some personal items missing from our room.
Tenemos algunos objetos personales desaparecidos de nuestra habitación.
Teh-NEH-mohs ahl-GOO-nohs ohb-HEH-tohs pehr-soh-NAH-lehs deh-sah-pah-reh-SEE-dohs deh NWEHS-trah ah-bee-tah-see-OHN

SPORTS AND EXERCISE

Can we walk faster?
¿Podemos caminar más rápido?
Poh-DEH-mohs kah-mee-NAHR mahs RRAH-pee-doh

Do you want to go to a drag racetrack?
¿Quieres ir a una pista de carreras?
Kee-EH-rehs eer ah OO-nah PEES-tah deh kah-REEH-rahs

Are you taking a walk?
¿Estás dando un paseo?
Ehs-TAHS DAHN-doh oon pah-SEH-oh

Do you want to jog for a kilometer or two?
¿Quieres trotar por uno o dos kilómetros?
Kee-EH-rehs troh-TAHR pohr OO-noh oh dohs kee-LOH-meh-trohs

How about fast walking?
¿Qué tal la caminata rápida?
Keh tahl lah kah-mee-NAH-tah RRAH-pee-dah

Would you like to walk with me?
¿Quisieras caminar conmigo?
Kee-see-EH-rahs kah-mee-NAHR kohn-MEE-goh

He is a really good player.
Él es un jugador realmente bueno.
Ehl ehs oon hoo-gah-DOHR reh-ahl-MEHN-teh BWEH-noh

I feel bad that they traded him to the other team.
Me siento mal porque ellos lo cambiaron al otro equipo.
Meh see-EHN-toh mahl POHR-keh EH-yohs loh kahm-bee-AH-rohn ahl
OH-troh eh-KEE-poh

Did you see that homerun?
¿Viste ese jonrón?
VEES-teh EH-seh hohn-RROHN

I have been a fan of that team for many years.
He sido fanático de ese equipo por muchos años
Eh SEE-doh fah-NAH-tee-koh deh EH-seh eh-KEE-poh pohr MOO-chohs
AH-nyohs

Who is your favorite team?
¿Cuál es tu equipo favorito?
Kwahl ehs too eh-KEE-poh fah-voh-REE-toh

Pele is my favorite player.
Pelé es mi jugador favorito.
Peh-LEH ehs mee hoo-gah-DOHR fah-voh-REE-toh

Do you like soccer?
¿Te gusta el fútbol?
Teh GOOS-tah ehl FOOT-bohl

Do you watch American football?
¿Ves fútbol americano?
Vehs FOOT-bohl ah-meh-ree-KAH-noh

Are there any games on right now?
¿Hay algunos partidos ahora mismo?
AH-ee ahl-GOO-NOHS pahr-TEE-dohs ah-OH-rah MEES-moh

That was a bad call by the ref.
Esa fue una mala decisión del árbitro.
EH-sah foo-EH OO-nah MAH-lah deh-see-see-OHN dehl AHR-bee-troh

I put a lot of money on this game.
Puse mucho dinero en este juego.
POO-seh MOO-choh dee-NEH-roh ehn EHS-teh hoo-EH-goh

His stats have been incredible this season.
Sus estadísticas han sido increíbles esta temporada.
Soos ehs-tah-DEES-tee-kahs ahn SEE-doh een-kreh-EE-blehs EHS-tah
tehm-poh-RAH-dah

Do you want to play baseball today?
¿Quieres jugar béisbol hoy?
Kee-EH-rehs hoo-GAHR BEH-ees-bohl OH-ee

Let's go to the soccer field and practice.
Vamos a practicar al campo de fútbol.
VAH-mohs ah prahk-tee-KAHR ahl KAHM-poh deh FOOT-bohl

I am barely working up a sweat.
Apenas me estoy esforzando.
Ah-PEH-nahs meh ehs-TOH-ee ehs-fohr-SAHN-doh

Let's go to the gym and lift weights.
Vamos al gimnasio y levantemos pesas.
VAH-mohs ahl heem-NAH-see-oh ee leh-vahn-TEH-mohs PEH-sahs

Give me more weights.
Dame más pesas.
DAH-meh mahs PEH-sahs

Take some weights off.
Quita algunas pesas.
KEE-tah ahl-GOO-nahs PEH-sahs

Will you spot me?
¿Me vas a ver?
Meh vahs ah vehr

How long do you want to run on the treadmill?
¿Cuánto tiempo quieres correr en la cinta?
KWAHN-toh tee-EHM-poh kee-EH-rehs koh-RREHR ehn lah SEEN-tah

Is this the best gym in the area?
¿Este es el mejor gimnasio en el área?
EHS-teh ehs ehl meh-HOHR heem-NAH-see-oh ehn ehl AH-reh-ah

Do I need a membership to enter this gym?
¿Necesito una membresía para entrar a este gimnasio?
Neh-seh-SEE-toh OO-nah mehm-breh-SEE-ah PAH-rah ehn-TRAHR ah
EHS-teh heem-NAH-see-oh

Do you have trial memberships for tourists?
¿Tienen membresías de prueba para turistas?
Tee-EH-nehn mehm-breh-SEE-ahs deh proo-EH-bah PAH-rah too-REES-tahs

My muscles are still sore from the last workout.
Aún me duelen los músculos por el último entrenamiento.
Ah-OON meh doo-EH-lehn lohs MOOS-koo-lohs pohr ehl OOL-tee-moh
ehn-treh-nah-mee-EHN-toh

Give me a second while I adjust this.
Dame un segundo mientras ajusto esto.
DAH-meh oon seh-GOON-doh mee-EHN-trahs ah-HOOS-toh EHS-toh

Time to hit the steam room!
¡Hora de ir al cuarto de vapor!
OH-rah deh eer ahl KWAHR-toh deh vah-POHR

You can put that in my locker.
Puedes poner eso en mi casillero.
PWEH-dehs poh-NEHR EH-soh ehn mee kah-see-YEH-roh

I think we have to take turns on this machine.
Creo que tenemos que tomar turnos en esta máquina.
KRE-oh keh teh-NEH-mohs keh toh-MAHR TOOR-nohs ehn EHS-tah
MAH-kee-nah

Make sure to wipe down the equipment when you are done.
Asegúrate de limpiar el equipo cuando termines.
Ah-seh-GOO-rah-teh deh leem-pee-AHR ehl eh-KEE-poh KWAHN-doh
tehr-MEE-nehs

Is there a time limit on working out here?
¿Hay un límite de tiempo para entrenar aquí?
AH-ee oon LEE-mee-teh deh tee-EHM-poh PAH-rah ehn-treh-NAHR ah-
KEE

We should enter a marathon.
Deberíamos entrar en una maratón.
Deh-beh-REE-ah-mohs ehn-TRAHR ehn OO-nah mah-rah-TOHN

How has your diet been going?
¿Cómo ha ido tu dieta?
KOH-moh ah EE-doh too dee-EH-tah

Are you doing keto?
¿Estás haciendo la dieta cetogénica?
Ehs-TAHS ah-see-EHN-doh lah dee-EH-tah seh-toh-HEH-nee-kah

Make sure to stay hydrated while you work out.
Asegúrate de mantenerte hidratado mientras entrenas.
Ah-seh-GOO-rah-teh deh mahn-teh-NEHR-teh ee-drah-TAH-doh mee-
EHN-trahs ehn-TREH-nahs

I'll go grab you a protein shake.
Iré a traerte un batido de proteína.
Ee-REH ah trah-EHR-teh oon bah-TEE-doh deh proh-teh-EE-nah

Do you want anything else? I'm buying.
¿Quieres algo más? Estoy comprando.
Kee-EH-rehs AHL-goh mahs. Ehs-TOH-ee kohm-PRAHN-doh

I need to buy some equipment before I play that.
Necesito comprar algunos equipos antes de jugar eso.
Neh-seh-SEE-toh kohm-PRAHR ahl-GOO-nohs eh-KEE-pohs AHN-tehs
deh hoo-GAHR EH-soh

Do you want to spar?
¿Quieres practicar combate?
Kee-EH-rehs prahk-tee-KAHR

Full contact sparring.
Combate de contacto pleno.
KOHM-BAH-teh deh kohn-TAHK-toh PLEH-noh

Just a simple practice round.
Solo una ronda de práctica.
SOH-loh OO-nah RROHN-dah deh PRAHK-tee-kah

Do you want to wrestle?
¿Quieres luchar?
Kee-EH-rehs loo-CHAHR

What are the rules to play this game?
¿Cuáles son las reglas para jugar este juego?
KWAH-lehs sohn lahs RREH-glahs PAH-rah hoo-GAHR EHS-teh hoo-EH-
goh

Do we need a referee?
¿Necesitamos un árbitro?
Neh-seh-see-TAH-mohs oon AHR-bee-troh

I don't agree with that call.
No estoy de acuerdo con esa decisión.
Noh ehs-TOH-ee deh ah-koo-EHR-doh kohn EH-sah deh-see-see-OHN

Can we get another opinion on that score?
¿Podemos obtener otra opinión sobre ese gol?
Poh-DEH-mohs ohb-teh-NEHR OH-trah oh-pee-nee-OHN SOH-breh EH-seh gohl

How about a game of table tennis?
¿Qué tal un juego de tenis de mesa?
Keh tahl oon hoo-EH-goh deh TEH-nees deh MEH-sah

Do you want to team up?
¿Quieres que formemos un equipo?
Kee-EH-rehs keh fohr-MEH-mohs oon eh-KEE-poh

Goal!
¡Gol!
Gohl

Homerun!
¡Jonrón!
Hohn-RROHN

Touchdown!
¡Anotación!
Ah-noh-tah-see-OHN

Score!
¡Gol!
¡Gohl!

On your mark, get set, go!
¡En sus marcas, listos, fuera!
Ehn soos MAHR-kahs, LEES-tohs, foo-EH-rah

Do you want to borrow my equipment?
¿Quieres que te preste mi equipo?
Kee-EH-rehs keh teh PREHS-teh mee eh-KEE-poh

Hold the game for a second.
Detén el juego un segundo.
Deh-TEHN ehl hoo-EH-goh oon seh-GOON-doh

I don't understand the rules of this game.
No entiendo las reglas de este juego.
Noh ehn-tee-EHN-doh lahs RREH-glahs deh EHS-teh hoo-EH-goh

Timeout!
¡Tiempo fuera!
Tee-EHM-poh foo-EH-rah

Can we switch sides?
¿Podemos cambiar de lados?
Poh-DEH-mohs kahm-bee-AHR deh LAH-dohs

There is something wrong with my equipment.
Algo está mal con mi equipo.
AHL-goh ehs-TAH mahl kohn mee eh-KEE-poh

How about another game?
¿Qué tal otro juego?
Keh tahl OH-troh hoo-EH-goh

I would like a do over of that last game.
Quisiera que repasáramos el último partido.
Kee-see-EH-rah keh rreh-pah-SAH-rah-mohs ehl OOL-tee-moh pahr-TEE-doh

Do you want to go golfing?
¿Quieres ir a jugar golf?
Kee-EH-rehs eer ah hoo-GAHR golf

Where can we get a golf cart?
¿Dónde podemos conseguir un carrito de golf?
DOHN-deh poh-DEH-mohs kohn-seh-GEER oon kah-RREE-toh deh golf

Do you have your own clubs?
¿Tienes tus propios palos?
Tee-EH-nehs toos PROH-pee-ohs PAH-lohs

Would you like to play with my spare clubs?
¿Te gustaría jugar con mis palos de repuesto?
Teh goos-tah-REE-ah hoo-GAHR kohn mees PAH-lohs deh rreh-PWEHS-toh

How many holes do you want to play?
¿Cuántos hoyos quieres jugar?
KWAHN-tohs OH-yohs kee-EH-rehs hoo-GAHR

Do I have to be a member of this club to play?
¿Tengo que ser miembro de este club para jugar?
TEHN-goh keh sehr mee-EHM-broh deh EHS-teh kloob PAH-rah hoo-GAHR

Let me ice this down, it is sore.
Déjame ponerle hielo a esto, está dolorido.
DEH-hah-meh poh-NEHR-leh ee-EH-loh ah EHS-toh, ehs-TAH doh-loh-REE-doh

I can't keep up with you, slow down.
No puedo seguirte el paso, ve más lento.
Noh PWEH-doh seh-GEER-teh ehl PAH-soh, veh mahs LEHN-toh

Let's pick up the pace a little bit.
Aceleremos un poco el ritmo.
Ah-seh-leh-REH-mohs oon POH-koh ehl REET-moh

Do you need me to help you with that?
¿Necesitas que te ayude con eso?
Neh-seh-SEE-tahs keh teh ah-YOO-deh kohn EH-soh

Am I being unfair?
¿Estoy siendo injusto?
Ehs-TOH-ee see-EHN-doh een-HOOS-toh

Let's switch teams for the next game.
Intercambiemos equipos para el próximo juego.
Een-tehr-kahm-bee-EH-mohs eh-KEE-pohs PAH-rah ehl PROHK-see-moh hoo-EH-goh

Hand me those weights.
Pásame esas pesas.
PAH-sah-meh EH-sahs PEH-sahs

THE FIRST 24 HOURS AFTER ARRIVING

When did you arrive?
¿Cuándo llegaste?
KWAHN-doh yeh-GAHS-teh

That was a very pleasant flight.
Ese fue un vuelo muy placentero.
EH-seh foo-EH oon voo-EH-loh MOO-ee plah-sehn-TEH-roh

Yes, it was a very peaceful trip. Nothing bad happened.
Sí, fue un viaje muy tranquilo. No pasó nada malo.
See, foo-EH oon vee-AH-heh MOO-ee trahn-KEE-loh. Noh pah-SOH NAH-dah MAH-loh

I have jetlag so need to lay down for a bit.
Tengo jetlag, así que necesito descansar por un rato.
TEHN-goh jetlag, ah-SEE keh neh-seh-SEE-toh dehs-kahn-SAHR pohr oon RRAH-toh

No, that was my first time flying.
No, esa fue mi primera vez volando.
Noh, EH-sah foo-EH mee pree-MEH-rah vehs voh-LAHN-doh

When is the check in time?
¿A qué hora es el ingreso?
Ah keh OH-rah ehs ehl een-GREH-soh

Do we need to get cash?
¿Necesitamos conseguir efectivo?
Neh-seh-see-TAH-mohs kohn-seh-GEER eh-fehk-TEE-voh

How much money do you have on you?
¿Cuánto dinero tienes encima?
KWAHN-toh dee-NEH-roh tee-EH-nehs ehn-SEE-mah

How long do you want to stay here?
¿Cuánto tiempo quieres quedarte aquí?
KWAHN-toh tee-EHM-poh kee-EH-rehs keh-DAHR-teh ah-KEE

Do we have all of our luggage?
¿Tenemos todo nuestro equipaje?
Teh-NEH-mohs TOH-doh NWEHS-troh eh-kee-PAH-heh

Let's walk around the city a bit before checking in.
Caminemos por la ciudad un poco antes de entrar al hotel.
Kah-mee-NEH-mohs pohr lah see-oo-DAHD oon POH-koh AHN-tehs deh
ehn-TRAHR ahl oh-TEHL

When is check in time for our hotel?
¿A qué hora es el ingreso a nuestro hotel?
Ah keh OH-rah ehs ehl een-GREH-soh ah NWEHS-troh oh-TEHL

I'll call the landlord and let him know we landed.
Llamaré al propietario para decirle que ya aterrizamos.
Yah-mah-REH ahl proh-pee-eh-TAH-ree-oh PAH-rah deh-SEER-leh keh
yah ah-teh-rree-SAH-mohs

Let's find a place to rent a car.
Encontraremos un lugar donde rentar un auto.
Ehn-kohn-tra-REH-mohs oon loo-GAHR DOHN-deh rrehn-TAHR oon AH-
oo-toh

Let's walk around the hotel room and make sure it's correct.
Caminemos por la habitación del hotel para asegurarnos de que sea la
correcta.
Kah-mee-NEH-mohs pohr lah ah-bee-tah-see-OHN dehl oh-TEHL PAH-
rah ah-seh-goo-RAHR-nohs deh keh SEH-ah lah koh-RREHK-tah

We'll look at our apartment and make sure everything is in order.
Revisaremos nuestro apartamento para asegurarnos de que todo está
en orden.
Rreh-vee-sah-REH-mohs NWEHS-troh ah-pahr-tah-MEHN-toh PAH-rah
ah-seh-goo-RAHR-nohs deh keh TOH-doh ehs-TAH ehn OHR-dehn

THE LAST 24 HOURS BEFORE LEAVING

Where are the passports?
¿Dónde están los pasaportes?
DOHN-deh ehs-TAHN lohs pah-sah-POHR-tehs

Did you fill out the customs forms?
¿Llenaste los formularios de aduana?
Yeh-NAHS-teh lohs fohr-moo-LAH-ree-ohs deh ah-doo-AH-nah

Make sure to pack everything.
Asegúrate de empacar todo.
Ah-seh-GOO-rah-teh deh ehm-pah-KAHR TOH-doh

Where are we going?
¿Adónde vamos?
Ah-DOHN-deh VAH-mohs

Which flight are we taking?
¿Qué vuelo estamos tomando?
Keh voo-EH-loh ehs-TAH-mohs toh-MAHN-doh

Check your pockets.
Revisa tus bolsillos.
Rreh-VEE-sah toos bohl-SEE-yohs

I need to declare some things for customs.
Necesito declarar algunas cosas en la aduana.
Neh-seh-SEE-toh deh-klah-RAHR ahl-GOO-nahs KOH-sahs ehn lah ah-doo-AH-nah

No, I have nothing to declare.
No, no tengo nada que declarar.
Noh, noh TEHN-goh NAH-dah keh deh-klah-RAHR

What is the checkout time?
¿A qué hora es la salida?
Ah keh OH-rah ehs lah sah-LEE-dah

Make sure your phone is charged.
Asegúrate de que tu celular esté cargado.
Ah-seh-GOO-rah-teh deh keh too seh-loo-LAHR ehs-TEH kahr-GAH-doh

Is there a fee attached to this?
¿Hay algún impuesto asociado esto?
AH-ee ahl-GOON eem-PWEHS-toh ah-soh-see-AH-doh ah EHS-toh

Do we have any outstanding bills to pay?
¿Tenemos algunas facturas pendientes por pagar?
Teh-NEH-mohs ahl-GOO-nahs fahk-TOO-rahs pehn-dee-EHN-tehs pohr pah-GAHR

What time does our flight leave?
¿A qué hora sale nuestro vuelo?
Ah keh OH-rah SAH-leh NWEHS-troh voo-EH-loh

What time do we need to be in the airport?
¿A qué hora necesitamos estar en el aeropuerto?
Ah keh OH-rah neh-seh-see-TAH-mohs ehs-TAHR ehn ehl ah-eh-roh-PWEHR-toh

How bad is the traffic going in the direction of the airport?
¿Qué tan malo es el tráfico yendo en dirección al aeropuerto?
Keh tahn MAH-loh ehs ehl TRAH-fee-koh YEHN-doh ehn dee-rehk-see-OHN ahl ah-eh-roh-PWEHR-toh

Are there any detours we can take?
¿Hay algunos desvíos que podamos tomar?
AH-ee ahl-GOO-nohs dehs-VEE-ohs keh poh-DAH-mohs toh-MAHR

What haven't we seen from our list since we've been down here?
¿Qué no hemos visto de nuestra lista desde que hemos llegado aquí?
Keh noh EH-mohs VEES-toh deh NWEHS-trah LEES-tah DEHS-deh keh EH-mohs yeh-GAH-doh ah-KEE

We should really buy some souvenirs here.
Realmente deberíamos comprar algunos souvenirs aquí.
Reh-ahl-MEHN-teh deh-beh-REE-ah-mohs kohm-PRAHR ahl-GOO-nohs souvenirs ah-KEE

Do you know any shortcuts that will get us there faster?
¿Conoces algunos atajos que nos lleven allá más rápido?
Koh-NOH-sehs ahl-GOO-nohs ah-TAH-hohs keh nohs YEH-vehn ah-YAH
mahs RAH-pee-doh

GPS the location and save it.
Busca la ubicación por GPS y guárdala.
BOOS-kah lah oo-bee-kah-see-OHN pohr heh peh eh-seh ee goo-AHR-
dah-lah

Are the items we're bringing back allowed on the plane?
¿Los objetos que traemos de vuelta están permitidos en el avión?
Lohs ohb-HEH-tohs keh trah-EH-mohs deh voo-EHL-tah ehs-TAHN pehr-
mee-TEE-dohs ehn ehl ah-vee-OHN

We should call our family back home before leaving.
Deberíamos llamar a nuestras familias allá en casa antes de irnos.
Deh-beh-REE-ah-mos yah-MAHR ah NWEHS-trahs fah-MEE-lee-ahs ah-
YAH ehn KAH-sah AHN-tehs deh EER-nohs

Make sure the pet cage is locked.
Asegúrate de que la jaula de mascotas esté cerrada.
Ah-see-GOO-rah-teh deh keh lah HA-oo-lah deh mahs-KOH-tahs ehs-TEH
seh-RRAH-dah

Go through your luggage again.
Revisa tu equipaje otra vez.
Rreh-VEE-sah too eh-kee-PAH-heh OH-trah vehs

MORE BOOKS BY LINGO MASTERY

Have you been trying to learn Spanish and simply can't find the way to expand your vocabulary?

Do your teachers recommend boring textbooks and complicated stories that you don't really understand?

Are you looking for a way to learn the language quicker without taking shortcuts?

If you answered *"Yes!"* to at least one of those previous questions, then this book is for you! We've compiled the **2000 Most Common Words in Spanish,** a list of terms that will expand your vocabulary to levels previously unseen.

Did you know that — according to an important study — learning the top two thousand (2000) most frequently used words will enable you to understand up to **84%** of all non-fiction and **86.1%** of fiction literature and **92.7%** of oral speech? Those are *amazing* stats, and this book will take you even further than those numbers!

In this book:

- A detailed introduction with tips and tricks on how to improve your learning
- A list of **2000** of the most common words in Spanish and their translations
- An example sentence for each word – in both Spanish *and* English
- Finally, a conclusion to make sure you've learned and supply you with a final list of tips

Don't look any further, we've got what you need right here!

In fact, we're ready to turn you into a Spanish speaker...

...are you ready to get involved in becoming one?

Do you know what the hardest thing for a Spanish learner is?

Finding PROPER reading material that they can handle...which is precisely the reason we've written this book!

Teachers love giving out tough, expert-level literature to their students, books that present many new problems to the reader and force them to search for words in a dictionary every five minutes — it's not entertaining, useful or motivating for the student at all, and many soon give up on learning at all!

In this book we have compiled 20 easy-to-read, compelling and fun stories that will allow you to expand your vocabulary and give you the tools to improve your grasp of the wonderful Spanish tongue.

How Spanish Short Stories for Beginners works:

- Each story will involve an important lesson of the tools in the Spanish language (Verbs, Adjectives, Past Tense, Giving Directions, and more), involving an interesting and entertaining story with realistic dialogues and day-to-day situations.
- The summaries follow: a synopsis in Spanish and in English of what you just read, both to review the lesson and for you to see if you understood what the tale was about.
- At the end of those summaries, you'll be provided with a list of the most relevant vocabulary involved in the lesson, as well as slang and sayings that you may not have understood at first

glance!

- Finally, you'll be provided with a set of tricky questions in Spanish, providing you with the chance to prove that you learned something in the story. Don't worry if you don't know the answer to any — we will provide them immediately after, but no cheating!

We want you to feel comfortable while learning the tongue; after all, no language should be a barrier for you to travel around the world and expand your social circles!

So look no further! Pick up your copy of **Spanish Short Stories for Beginners** and improve your Spanish right now!

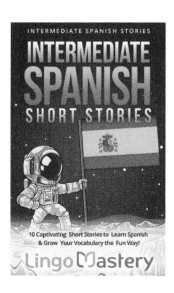

**Improve your Spanish skills and grow your vocabulary
with these 10 entertaining Spanish short stories!**

The best part of learning a new language is experiencing the culture and diving into activities that will enrich your life and vocabulary. The best way to learn a new language is by reading, and in this Spanish book you will find yourself turning page after page to get to the end of each captivating story that will engage your mind and help you improve your Spanish.

In this book you will find:

- **10 captivating short stories** that develop in circumstances such as traveling, personal relationships, among other topics that you will find easy to relate to.
- The stories are broken down into manageable chapters, so you always make progress with the story.
- Carefully written stories with you as an **intermediate level reader in mind**, using straightforward grammar and commonly used words so you can enjoy reading while learning new grammatical structures without being overwhelmed.
- **Plenty of natural dialogues** in each story that you would actually use in an everyday conversation, which will drastically improve your speaking and comprehension ability at the same time!

- At the end of each chapter there will be a comprehensive guide specially designed for intermediate level readers, it will take you through a summary of each story followed by a vocabulary of some of the words from the story to make sure that you understand the story fully.

Chapter by chapter you will find yourself effortlessly reading each story. Not struggling like in basic textbooks or boring reads. You will get involved by reading the dialogue of the characters by learning how to express yourself in different contexts and more importantly by learning new Spanish words that will get you closer to your goal of becoming fully conversational!

Enjoy the book and Buena Suerte!

Lingo Mastery

Is conversational Spanish turning a little too tricky for you? Do you have no idea on how to order a meal or book a room at a hotel?

If your answer to any of the previous questions was 'Yes', then this book is for you!

If there's even been something tougher than learning the grammar rules of a new language, it's finding the way to speak with other people in that tongue. Any student knows this – we can try our best at practicing, but you always want to avoid making embarrassing mistakes or not getting your message through correctly.

'How do I get out of this situation?' Many students ask themselves, to no avail, but no answer is forthcoming.

Until now.

We have compiled **MORE THAN ONE HUNDRED** Spanish Stories for Beginners along with their translations, allowing new Spanish speakers to have the necessary tools to begin studying how to set a meeting, rent a car or tell a doctor that they don't feel well! We're not wasting time here with conversations that don't go anywhere: if you want to know how to solve problems (while learning a ton of Spanish along the way, obviously), this book is for you!

How Conversational Spanish Dialogues works:

- Each new chapter will have a fresh, new story between two people who wish to solve a common, day-to-day issue that you will surely encounter in real life.
- A Spanish version of the conversation will take place first, followed by an English translation. This ensures that you fully understood just what it was that they were saying!
- Before and after the main section of the book, we shall provide you with an introduction and conclusion that will offer you important strategies, tips and tricks to allow you to get the absolute most out of this learning material.
- That's about it! Simple, useful and incredibly helpful; you will **NOT** need another conversational Spanish book once you have begun reading and studying this one!

We want you to feel comfortable while learning the tongue; after all, no language should be a barrier for you to travel around the world and expand your social circles!

So look no further!

Pick up your copy of **Conversational Spanish Dialogues** and start learning Spanish right now!

CONCLUSION

Congratulations! You have reached the end of this book and learned over **1,500** ways to express yourself in the Spanish language! It is a moment to celebrate, since you are now much closer to achieving complete fluency of the Spanish tongue.

However, the learning simply cannot end here – you may have unlocked a massive amount of incredibly useful day-to-day phrases that will get you anywhere you need to go, but are you prepared to use them correctly? Furthermore, will you remember them during your travels when faced with one of the situations we've presented in this book?

Only by continuously studying the material found in previous chapters will you ever be able to summon the words and phrases encountered above, since it isn't a matter of *what* the phrases are, but *how* and *when* to use them. Knowing the exact context is crucial, as well as reinforcing your knowledge with other materials.

For this reason, we have created a quick list of tips to make the most of this Spanish Phrasebook and expanding your vocabulary and grasp of the Spanish language:

1. **Practice every day:** You can be very good at something thanks to the gift of natural talent, but practice is the only way to *stay* good. Make sure to constantly pick up the book and read the words, saying them out loud and taking note of your mistakes so you can correct them.
2. **Read while listening:** A very popular and modern way of learning a new language is by using the RwL (reading while listening) method. It has proven that this method can greatly boost fluency, help you ace language tests and improve your learning in other subjects. Feel free to try out our audiobooks and other listening materials in Spanish– you'll love them!
3. **Studying in groups:** It's always best to go on an adventure together – even if it's a language adventure! You'll enjoy

yourself more if you can find someone who wants to learn with you. Look to friends, your partner, your family members or colleagues for support, and maybe they can even help you make the process easier and quicker!

4. **Creating your own exercises:** This book provides you with plenty of material for your learning processes, and you will probably be happy with reading it every time you can... however, you need to increase the difficulty by looking for other words and phrases in the Spanish language which you don't know the pronunciation to, and trying to decipher it for yourself. Use the knowledge you've gained with previous lessons and discover entirely new words!

With that said, we have now fully concluded this Spanish Phrasebook which will surely accelerate your learning to new levels. Don't forget to follow every tip we've included, and to keep an eye out for our additional Spanish materials.